Pronunciation in Action

P9-DFO-723

Other titles in this series include:

Pronunciation in Action

LINDA TAYLOR

Prentice Hall

New York   London   Toronto   Sydney   Tokyo   Singapore

PRENTICE HALL INTERNATIONAL ENGLISH LANGUAGE TEACHING

First published 1993 by
Prentice Hall International (UK) Ltd
Campus 400, Maylands Avenue
Hemel Hempstead
Hertfordshire HP2 7EZ
A division of
Simon & Schuster International Group

© Prentice Hall International (UK) Ltd, 1993

All rights reserved. No part of this publication may be
reproduced, stored in a retrieval system, or transmitted,
in any form, or by any means, electronic, mechanical,
photocopying, recording or otherwise, without prior
permission, in writing, from the publisher.
For permission within the United States of America
contact Prentice Hall Inc., Englewood Cliffs, NJ 07632.

Typeset in 10½/12½pt Times
by Fakenham Photosetting Ltd, Fakenham

Printed and bound in Great Britain
by Redwood Books Ltd, Trowbridge, Wiltshire

Library of Congress Cataloging-in-Publication Data

Taylor, Linda (Linda L.)
    Pronunciation in action / Linda Taylor.
      p. cm.
    ISBN 0–13–017864–0 (pbk)
      1. English language-Pronunciation-Study and
teaching.
  I. Title.
  PE1137.T39 1993
  428.1′07–dc20   93–14344
                           CIP

British Library Cataloguing in Publication Data

A catalogue record for this book is available from
the British Library
ISBN 0–13–017864–0 (Pbk)

---

1 2 3 4 5 96 95 94 93

Contents

Indexes

Acknowledgements

I would like to thank my Students at Clarendon College, Nottingham, who provided the stimulus for these activities, and who tried them out in class. My thanks are also due to Isobel Fletcher de Tellez for her help and hard work in getting the manuscript of this book into shape.

I am grateful to the following for permission to reproduce copyright material: The British Broadcasting Corporation and The Richard Stone Partnership for permission to use David Croft's material from the television series, ''Allo 'Allo'. Hodder and Stoughton Limited Sevenoaks, Kent for permission to use the phoneme frequency chart from A.C. Gimson, *An Introduction to the Pronuciation of English*. Random House UK Ltd for permission to use Gavin Ewart's poem, 'a really hot meal', and John Cooper Clark's 'Nothing'. Campbell Connelly & Co. Limited for permission to use 'The Hokey Cokey', Mercury Records for permission to use the lyrics from the INXS song, 'Mediate' Nottingham Weekly Recorder and Post for the article on UFO's from Issue 517.

The author and publishers have made every effort to trace and acknowledgc ownership of copyright. Suitable arrangements can be made with any copyright holders whom it has not been possible to contact.

INTRODUCTION

Structure and content

Pronunciation in Action is a book of ready-made lesson ideas which focus on pronunciation. I have met many teachers who are wary of tackling pronunciation in class, in the mistaken belief that to do so needs vast theoretical knowledge and practical expertise. This book sets out to 'demystify' the subject, and to show that teaching 'pron' is great fun, and much simpler than you think.

Some of the activities in this book are aimed at a very specific target, such as the articulation of a single sound. Others are aimed more generally at helping students to become aware not only of *what* they are saying, but of *how* they are saying it, taking into account the effect this may have on their hearers.

The book is divided into four sections, each of which is devoted to one aspect of pronunciation and contains activities to provide practice in the chosen aspect. An introduction at the beginning of each of these four sections explains in some detail the particular aspect concerned. The introduction also explains the rationale behind the activities in the section, together with a guide to their content. The four sections are:

1. Working with English pronunciation in context

Some of the areas covered in this section are:
- the 'Englishness' of English
- improving accurate listening
- improving students' self-monitoring
- improving students' discrimination of sounds made by others
- emotions and how they affect what is said
- the use of gesture, mime and emphasis
- some forces at work in rapid spoken English (e.g. contractions)

2. Working with English sounds

The activities in this section contain material for:
- sound discrimination practice
- introducing phonemic script
- practising phonemic script
- using mnemonics to aid recall of sounds

- using students' own examples of sounds in context
- working with sound spelling relationships
- practising tongue twisters

3. Working with English rhyme and rhythm

This section deals with word stress, including compounds and multi-syllabic words. It also exploits rhyme and rhythm through poems, jingles, limericks and raps, using:
- rhyming work cards
- jigsaw activities
- snap and bingo games
- matching rhyming words
- action rhymes and songs

4. Working with English intonation

There are ideas here for lessons on:
- shifting stress and how this affects meaning
- notation of stress patterns
- vocal range
- accurate stress placement and pausing, and their effect on oral fluency
- miming intonation patterns with hands and bodies
- falling tones and their relationship to new information
- rising tones and their relationship to shared information
- socialising and the use of rising tones
- the relationship between intonation and punctuation
- intonation and text type
- intonation in lists, questions and contradictions

Methodology

This book provides activities for individual, pair, group and whole class work. All of the activities are task-based. Flanking the central, practical task there is an introductory warm-up phase and a follow-up phase. The three phases may take different forms, as the five examples below will show.

Warm up	Task	Follow up
1. Learners enact scenario to be focus of main task	Learners listen to native speakers enacting same scenario	Learners study transcript and mark text for feature practised
2. Teacher demonstrates team game	Teacher plays team game with whole class	Team game played in groups, simultaneously, teacher monitors only
3. Learners given questions, groups brainstorm responses	Pairs of learners try out questions and answers using feature to be practised	Chosen pairs act out dialogues, teacher corrects feature as needed
4. Teacher plays taped dialogue, learners listen without script	Intensive work on dialogue with transcript	Guessing game based on dialogue
5. Teacher dictates gapped text	Group or pair discussions of possible fillers for gaps	Whole class discussion of possibilities

There are many activity types in this book including:
- worksheets and work card completion
- choral singing and reciting
- brainstorming
- discrimination and classification exercises
- dictation
- gap filling
- crosswords and wordsearches
- problem solving
- milling activities
- making and responding to questions
- team games, card games, dice games, board games, matching games
- role enactment and drama
- imitation and repetition
- dialogue construction and reading
- mime
- discussion

- self and peer correction
- listening to native speaker models
- text marking
- giving speeches and presentations
- paired 'information gap' activities
- poetry writing.

In order to make the best use of *Pronunciation in Action*, you should read through the introduction to each section first. You will then be in a position to know which sections and which activities will suit your learners best. The Index will also help you to locate suitable activities: it gives summaries of each activity in the book, and indicates which activities are suitable for young learners, teenagers or adults at elementary, intermediate or advanced level. There is a 'Teacher's Diary' space at the end of each activity for your comments on the response of your learners, on useful aspects of the activity, and on the revisions you would make for future sessions in which you might use the same input. Each individual activity is prefaced by an indication as to its target level, age, and purpose. Detailed steps are given to teachers for both preparation and execution of the activity, often with sample teaching material. The Appendices at the back of this book give reference material relevant to the four sections of the book.

Further reading

Below is a short list of works which I have found useful in compiling *Pronunciation in Action* and which I would recommend as further reading. The list is not meant to be exhaustive, but represents the range of student's books and teacher's resource and reference material available at present. It has to be said that this range is not yet extensive. However, pronunciation seems to be gaining in popularity as an area of study and of teaching, so I hope more titles will become available soon.

Books for teachers

David Brazil, *The Communicative Value of Intonation in English*, English Language Research (University of Birmingham), 1985.
A thorough account, with accompanying tape cassette, of David Brazil's widely acclaimed system of classifying intonation patterns. It discusses five main areas: Prominence; Key and Termination; Tone; Pitch Sequence; and Orientation; giving copious examples. This work does not merely explain *what* patterns are used in English, but attempts to explain *why* speakers may choose one rather than another.

G. Brown, *Listening to Spoken English* (2nd edn), Longman, 1990.
A very readable and insightful account of the processes at work in spoken English and their relationship to English spelling. Through explaining the features of pronunciation, it aims to help learners understand the English they hear.

A.C. Gimson, *An Introduction to the Pronunciation of English*, Edward Arnold, 1980.
The classic reference book on pronunciation, this is an invaluable resource for teachers. It is divided into three sections: Speech and Language; The Sounds of English; and The Word and Connected Speech.

Daniel Jones, *English Pronunciation Dictionary*, ed. A. Gimson (14th edn), Cambridge University Press, 1991.

Joanne Kenworthy, *Teaching English Pronunciation*, Longman, 1987.
This popular book has an optional cassette. It contains a wealth of teaching tips and has useful tables of rules for weak forms, linkage, stress, and spellings. Part Two of the book lists common pronunciation problems of learners from nine language backgrounds.

Charles W. Kreidler, *The Pronunciation of English*, Blackwell, 1989.
A very comprehensive reference work in fourteen sections, some of which contain interesting material not found elsewhere, notably on phonotactics and on phonological processes in speech. It is an interactive work, which leads the reader through many integral exercises to discover facts and apply concepts. (Keys to the exercises are provided.)

Peter Roach, *English Phonetics and Phonology*, Cambridge University Press, 1991.
A highly readable and approachable book, which gives the main facts and theoretical issues in phonetics and phonology, this book is used in many universities and higher education establishments by teachers of EFL in training. The accompanying recorded material gives exercises in pronunciation, discrimination and transcription.

Michael Swan and Bernard Smith, *Learner English*, Cambridge University Press, 1987.
This is a detailed contrastive analysis of the problems of learners of English from nineteen different language backgrounds. Orthography, grammar and vocabulary are treated as well as pronunciation. It is an essential 'item of luggage' for TEFL teachers working abroad, and especially for those teaching monolingual groups of learners.

John Wells, *Longman Pronouncing Dictionary*, Longman, 1989.

In addition to these books for teachers, I would draw the reader's attention to Brita Haycraft's slot in each issue of the magazine *Practical English Teaching* (Mary Glasgow Publications) which has brainteaser-type questions (with key) on pronunciation matters.

Finally, I would urge those interested in the teaching of pronunciation to read *Speak Out*, the journal of the Phonology Special Interest Group of the International Association of Teachers of English as a Foreign Language.

Books for students

Ann Baker, *Tree or Three*, Cambridge University Press, 1982; Ann Baker, *Ship or Sheep*, Cambridge University Press, 1981.
These two books have become standard works for students, the first for elementary learners and the second for intermediate learners. They can be used alongside any course book, and are ideal for self-access. There is a teacher's guide to these two titles, called *Introducing English Pronunciation*, by the same author and publisher.

Bill Bowler, Sarah Cunningham and Sue Parminter, *Headway Pronunciation*, Oxford University Press, 1991.
Three new pronunciation titles have now been produced to accompany the *Headway* Pre-intermediate, Intermediate and Upper Intermediate course books. They deal with individual sounds, stress, connected speech and intonation and can be used with any course, not just the *Headway* series.

Barbara Bradford, *Intonation in Context*, Cambridge University Press, 1988.
This book is designed for upper intermediate and advanced students and gives practice in aspects of David Brazil's system. Its main strength lies in its extension of the more usual repetition and practice exercises to some genuinely communicative activities. There is a teacher's book and cassette tape to accompany the material, which is designed for class use but which is also capable of being followed as a self-access course if used in conjunction with the teacher's book.

Robert Hooke and Judith Rowell, *A Handbook of English Pronunciation*, Nelson, 1982.
A vastly underrated book, this is a comprehensive handbook with extensive recorded material. Its clear descriptions, illustrated by photographs of the mouth, together with the wealth of exercises to practise each feature, make it a very approachable course for any learner at intermediate level and above. The pair and group work built into the course is ideal for class exploitation. However, this is a course which can easily be used by students working alone.

Colin Mortimer, *Elements of Pronunciation*, Cambridge University Press, 1985.

This course is a compilation of five previously published booklets which have been re-edited. In particular, the tape recordings are now very easy to use for self-access purposes. It progresses from initial practice with individual words and phrases taken out of the dialogues, to repetition and practice of whole chunks of dialogue. Stress, weak forms, contractions, consonant clusters and linking are the subjects of study. These witty dialogues are designed for use with upper intermediate and advanced learners.

J.D. O'Connor and C. Fletcher, *Sounds English*, Longman, 1989.

This is a book for intermediate learners. It is divided into sections nominally devoted to single vowels or consonant sounds. However, there is also much material for practising intonation, weak forms, stress and linking. The presentation is lively, with line drawings, tables, maps and charts. Many of the exercises are for pair and group exploitation, making this a classroom text rather than a self-study course. However, the taped material would be useful for students working through the sections again at home. Two appealing features of the course are the 'sound-spelling boxes' provided for each sound, and the chart at the front of the book which lists problems of various language backgrounds and names the units dealing with these problems.

SECTION I

WORKING WITH ENGLISH PRONUNCIATION IN CONTEXT

Introduction

In order for our learners to improve their pronunciation, they must perceive a *need* to do so: part of our job as teachers should therefore be to raise learners' awareness of shortcomings in their pronunciation. It is extremely sad to hear fluent speakers who have attained a high level of proficiency in other aspects of English, yet whose accent renders them unintelligible. How galling it must be for them to find themselves constantly asked to repeat what they have said. And how often do L2 speakers find their requests refused because the intonation patterns they use give faulty signals?

Some questions we could ask to help learners to think about the effect that accent has on listeners are:[1]

- How do they respond to a non-native speaker who mispronounces their own language?
- What do they think of when 'pronunciation' is mentioned?
- Which sounds in their language do non-native speakers find hard to pronounce?
- Which sounds in English do they find hard to pronounce? What about stress and intonation difficulties?
- Are there some circumstances in which they would make more of an effort with their English accent than others?

I believe there are three main areas to concentrate on, in trying to raise learners' awareness of their own pronunciation:

1. Firstly, it is important for them to have a sense of the 'Englishness of English'. Exposure to monologues, such as cassette recordings of stories or lectures, is important as the situational dialogues that are common in coursebooks often proceed in short utterances, which do not always give much sense of the overall rhythm and sounds of English.[2] Soundless videos can be watched and imitated to show how English people use their lips and mouths when they speak. The particular position taken up by the vocal organs varies according to the language spoken and is known as 'articulatory setting'. As Honikman has observed, 'Where two languages are disparate in articulatory setting, it is not possible to master the pronunciation of one whilst maintaining the articulatory setting of the other.'[3] To prepare for looking and sounding English, Honikman advises learners to

taper and concave the tongue, draw it back into the mouth so that the tongue tip or blade is against the alveolar ridge, close the jaws without clenching, keep the lips still, then swallow to relax. She also suggests saying the sounds /t/, /d/, /n/, /l/ to 'limber up for English'. Activities 1, 2, 3, 4, 6, 7 and 12 are designed to introduce learners to the 'Englishness of English'.

2. Secondly, learners need to learn to listen accurately. So much of the information we take in these days is absorbed through the visual channel, whereas, in order to improve pronunciation, learners need to have ears which are sensitive to sounds. Two useful exercises to develop sensitivity are: closing the eyes and listening to sounds outside the classroom, then inside the classroom for a set time and then noting them down; and listening to music to decide how many instruments are playing at one time.[4] Activities 1, 2, 3, 6, 9, 10 are designed to develop listening skills.[5]

3. Finally, learners need to monitor their own performance. This can be done by comparing it with models of native English speech, and also by speaking in English to native speakers or to non-natives from other linguistic backgrounds. Activities 5, 8, 9, 10, 11, 12 are devoted to self-evaluation and monitoring.

Notes
1. Joanne Kenworthy has devised a useful questionnaire for just this purpose, see *Teaching English Pronunciation* under Further reading in the Introduction to this book.
2. Three British companies marketing books with cassettes are: **Morley Audio Services**, Elmfield Road, Morley, Leeds, LS27 0NN; **Ulversoft Soundings**, The Green, Bradgate Road, Anstey, Leicester, LE7 7FU; and **Isis Oasis Audio Books**, 55 St Thomas Street, Oxford, OX1 1JG.
3. Beatrice Honikman, 'Articulatory Settings', in D. Abercrombie (ed.), *In Honour of Daniel Jones*, papers contributed on the occasion of his 80th birthday, 12 September 1961, Longman, 1964.
4. I am grateful to Claire Morris of Western Language Centre, Kemble, for these ideas.
5. For more listening activities, see M. Rost, *Listening In Action*, Prentice Hall, 1991.

1 Mr Brown says, 'Yes'

Level	Intermediate
Students	Teenage to adult
Groups	Whole class or group
Purpose	To convey attitude by varying the way the voice is used, whilst keeping the words the same
Text type	Title phrase

In this activity

Learners play a guessing game to reveal the importance of pronunciation in conveying attitude.

Preparation

Write a list of 'feeling' words on the board. A possible list is provided in the Sample teaching material below.

Procedure

1. Write the 'feeling' words on the board and also write each one on a slip of paper. Demonstrate the game to the class: take a slip of paper yourself and do not show it to the class. Then say the phrase, Mr. Brown says 'Yes', in the manner of the 'feeling' word you have on the slip of paper in front of you. Invite your learners to guess which word you were demonstrating. Whoever guesses correctly then takes up the game. Show this learner, secretly, another slip of paper which must be demonstrated to the rest of the class in the way that you have just shown. The learner who guesses this second word then continues the game, and so on.

2. Follow up: Groups of learners can play the game simultaneously.

Sample teaching material

List of 'feeling' words: pleased   furious   afraid   ecstatic
disgusted   smug   shocked   embarrassed   shy   miserable
worried   confused   upset

Teacher's diary

Were the learners able to identify the feeling successfully? If so, was
this because of gesture rather than vocal quality? Try tape recording
the phrase and see if there is equal success.

2 Say it with feeling

Level	Intermediate to advanced
Students	Adult
Groups	Groups
Purpose	To practise conveying different attitudes by varying vocal quality, pitch, loudness, range, intonation, etc.
Text type	Students' own spoken texts

In this activity

Learners play a game involving matching voice with attitude.

Preparation

You will need a die for each group of learners, and a list of six 'feeling' words taken from the list in the Sample teaching material.

Procedure

1. Ask your learners to prepare a short talk about themselves. It can include where they are from, where they went to school, stories about their childhood, information about home and family, information about their town and country, their hopes for the future, etc. One paragraph will be sufficient.

2. Check the students' work for errors, correcting as necessary.

3. Divide the learners into groups and give each group a die and a list of six 'feeling' words, numbered to correspond with the die throws.

4. Demonstrate the game with one group whilst the other groups look on: the first player throws the die, then delivers his or her prepared talk according to the 'feeling' he has thrown. For example, if 'bored' corresponds to the

number three and he or she throws a three, then the talk must be delivered in a bored way, and so on.

5. Set the groups to work on the game simultaneously. Monitor the groups, giving help as needed.

6. After everyone has had a minimum of three turns at speaking, stop the game and call on two or three of the most convincing speakers to demonstrate different 'feeling' words. Discuss with the class why they were so successful and point out some of their vocal features, such as range, pitch variation, intonation, etc.

7. Follow up: Work with learners in a similar way on dialogues, which must be read in different ways (e.g. amorously, sadly).

Sample teaching material

Choose six words from this list to use in the game. Groups can have the same six words, or each group can have different sets.

pleased	elated	glad	calm
uneasy	grieved	comfortable	silly
contented	satisfied	embarrassed	cautious
bored	hesitant	scared	fearful
surprised	confident	daring	eager
uncomfortable	confused	angry	anxious
lonely	tired	discontented	excited
warm	solemn	frustrated	stubborn
relieved	hopeful	serious	apathetic
proud	despairing	energetic	annoyed
flustered	cross	foolish	jealous
kind	miserable	stupid	tense
inadequate	shocked	troubled	relaxed
trapped	weepy	loving	wonderful
happy	peaceful	awkward	flat

Teacher's diary

Was there any evidence that learners were improving in their ability to alter vocal features in a suitable way?

3 Act English

Level	Intermediate to advanced
Students	Teenage to adult
Groups	Whole class and groups or pairs
Purpose	To show learners some of the features of English 'accent'
Text type	Learners' own autobiographies

In this activity

Learners talk about themselves in their own language, using an English accent, then discuss its features.

Preparation

None.

Procedure

1. Ask your learners, working individually, to write a short biography of themselves, for example, by completing the following:

   My name is _____. I was born in _____ and I live in _____. I have
   _____ brothers and _____ sisters. The things I like most are _____.
   The things I don't like very much are _____.

   This biography should be written in the learners' native language.

2. Ask the learners to work in pairs or groups to read out their biographies to each other *in an English accent* but using their own language. The other students in the pairs or groups listen and note as many ways as they can in which the English accent is different from their own. If you have a multi-lingual group, this is not so easy, but should still be interesting.

3. Ask two or three learners to read their biographies out loud, before asking the class to volunteer their observations. List these, and your own, on the board.

Teacher's diary

Did the learners volunteer any ideas which you had not thought of?
Did the exercise help the learners to decide priorities for improving their own English accents?

---

4 Wordless video

Level	Intermediate and above
Students	All ages
Groups	Whole class, pairs or groups
Purpose	To show the relationship between *what* is said and *how* it is said
Text type	Teacher's chosen video clips

In this activity

Learners mime, then put words to soundless videos.

Preparation

Choose some video clips which you feel exemplify English speech well – situations in which surprise or anger is expressed are ideal.[1]

Procedure

1. Tell your learners that you are going to show them a video clip without the sound, and that afterwards they will have to re-enact the clip. Play the video clip.

2. Divide the learners into pairs or groups corresponding to the number of protagonists in the chosen video. Their task is to act out what they saw, using only nonsense syllables – the traditional word to use is 'rhubarb, rhubarb, rhubarb, . . .'

3. Now ask the learners to go through the same exercise, but this time to put English words to it – you will probably need to play the video two or three more times, so that the learners can do this.

4. Ask some of the learners to act out what they have worked on, and make a note of any particularly well pronounced (or, alternatively, erroneous) English features.

5. Finally, play the video clip with its sound track, and discuss salient features of pronunciation, such as range, stress and intonation, as well as individual sounds which learners may have mispronounced.

6. Follow the same procedure with the other video clips you have chosen.

Teacher's diary

Did this activity throw up pronunciation difficulties which you had not discovered before? How close did your learners come to imitating the clip correctly?

Note

1. For more ideas on using video in class, see B. Tomalin and S. Stempleski, *Video in Action*, Prentice Hall, 1990.

5 Hard sell

Level	Elementary to advanced
Students	All ages
Groups	Pairs or groups
Purpose	To show the relationship between what we say and how we say it
Text type	Learners' advertisements

In this activity

Learners play the role of TV or radio advertiser, trying to sell a product.

Preparation

If possible, find authentic TV or radio advertisements in English, or alternatively use newspaper advertisements or authentic advertisements used in English coursebooks. Bring your chosen video cassette recording or newspaper advertisements to class. Also, bring some real objects which might be advertised in the media.

Procedure

1. Before you present the advertisements to the class, tell your learners that you are going to show them some English advertisements and what the products are. Ask your learners to suggest what the advertisements might say about the products, then show the advertisements.

2. Set out your real objects on a table in front of the class – you can also use pictures of objects, such as a car (which would be impossible to bring to class!). Invite your learners to choose an object which they would like to sell, and divide the class into groups according to the object they have chosen.

3. Set the groups to work, deciding what they are going to say in a TV or radio advertisement for their object. Set a time limit for the task.

4. After the allotted time, invite each group to record on tape – or videotape – the advertisement they have been working on. When each group has spoken its advertisement, you will then have a complete 'commercial break' of several advertisements running one after the other.

5. Working with the class as a whole, tell your learners that they are now going to hear all the advertisements, and they must decide which is the most convincing, and which the most boring. Their decision must not be made on the basis of how interesting or boring the *product* is, but on the basis of how interesting or boring the *speakers* are! Which advertisement do they think will actually sell the product? Play the tape.

6. Find out from the groups which advertisements worked well or badly for them, and why. Hopefully, part of the reason will be the use of stress and intonation – if not, you will have to point these features out yourself.

7. Invite the unsuccessful advertisers to try out their advertisements again, varying the intonation and stress to sound more interested in what they are selling.

Teacher's diary

Were the groups of learners able to hear why some of the class sounded more interested than others? Were they able to suggest how improvements could be made?

6 Spotting contractions

Level	Intermediate to advanced
Students	Teenage to adult
Groups	Whole class, pairs or groups
Purpose	To show learners how often contractions are used in English speech
Text type	Teacher's authentic spoken extract

In this activity

Learners listen to authentic English speech and discover where contractions occur.

Preparation

Find an extract of authentic English speech or use the Sample teaching material.

Procedure

1. Write on the board some sentences in which contractions might occur in spoken English;

   e.g. Where is he going?, He has given me the book, What do you recommend?, I do not know.

   Ask your learners to say how these would be spoken in rapid colloquial style.

   Answer: Where's he going?, He's given me the book, What d'you recommend?, I don't know.

2. Tell your learners that you are going to play them a recording of some English speakers. They will be given the transcript, but the contracted

forms are blanked out. Their task is to listen, and complete the text. Give out the gapped transcript.

3. Play the recording once, then ask learners to confer in pairs or groups to see how they have filled the gaps. Play the recording again if required.

4. With the class as a whole, check answers. If there are points in the transcript where contractions *could* have occurred but *didn't*, can the learners suggest why contractions were not made? (In the Sample teaching material, the first line does not show a contraction because the speaker is reading out a written question, and in the last line there is contrastive stress on 'is'.)

5. Follow up: The rap, 'Hello there now', from Activity 7 might be appropriate material to use in a follow-up lesson.

Sample teaching material

Tapescript 114d from *Collins Cobuild English Course Level 2*[1]

SB: Where is he going? Can you guess why?
CM: He__ going to Epsom because it__ Derby Day. Or is it –? He does mention that it__ Derby Day.
SB: Yes, that__ probably why he__ going. And he says he__ going for the races. But he__ not going to bet, on horses. And he__ not going to watch them run. And he__ not even working the betting machines.
CM: So what is he going for?
SB: Maybe he__ a pickpocket.

Teacher's diary

Were the learners able to complete the gaps? Did you ask them to read the transcript to each other afterwards? If you did, were the learners able to use the contractions themselves, or did they slip back into the full forms?

Note
1. The sample material is from D. Willis and J. Willis, *Cobuild English Course Level 2*, 1989, Tape Exercise 114d. This course has unscripted recordings which are an invaluable source of good quality authentic spoken English.

7 English as she is spoke

Level	Intermediate and above
Students	Adults
Groups	Whole class, pairs or groups
Purpose	To show learners the effect of common elisions and assimilations on the way English is spoken as opposed to written
Text type	Teacher's word lists, and play-on-words jokes

In this activity

Students relate the sound of phrases to their spelling, and try to 'find the joke' in some sample plays-on-words.

Preparation

Find your own examples of elisions and assimilations, or use the sample phrases. ('Elision' is where a sound is missing altogether as in *Chris(t)mas*, and 'assimilation' is where one sound merges into the next as in *hambag* for *hand-bag*.) Find some English jokes which depend on these features for their punch-line, or use the Sample teaching material.

Procedure

1. Tell your learners that you are going to give out a list of English words and phrases which do not look like English because they are spelt exactly as they would be pronounced, not as they would be spelt normally.

2. Divide the class into pairs or groups and distribute the list. Set a time limit for the task you have outlined – about five minutes should be ample.

3. Subdivide the groups and ask them to form new groups to confirm what they decided in their old groups, before giving the answers in open class.

4. Using the overhead projector if available, show your chosen plays-on-words jokes and invite your learners, working as a class, to say why they are funny. Give the explanations, as required, then ask pairs of learners to practise telling jokes to other pairs.

5. Follow up: The rap, 'Hello there now', which is reproduced below, could be sung as consolidation work, since it shows many elisions and assimilations. The rhythm is four beats to a bar. I find it works well if students slap knees on beats one and two, clap on beat three, then rest on beat four:

slap slap clap rest

Sample teaching material

List of words and phrases[1]

1. GrapeBritain	9. WesGermany	17. cllective
2. stapement	10. aspecs	18. pliticl
3. hundrebpounds	11. thefacthat	19. cabnet
4. Iwongkgo	12. asconfusasever	20. chancllor
5. armourgcar	13. NorthernIrelan-	21. simlar
6. Ivebeeng-	troubles	22. libry
concentrating	14. nothingstanstill	23. secrtry
7. firsthree	15. intrest	24. govnor
8. lasyear	16. diffrent	25. medcne

Key

1. Great Britain	9. West Germany	17. collective
2. statement	10. aspects	18. political
3. hundred pounds	11. the fact that	19. cabinet
4. I won't go	12. as confused as ever	20. chancellor
5. armoured car	13. Northern Ireland	21. similar
6. I've been	troubles	22. library
concentrating	14. nothing stands still	23. secretary
7. first three	15. interest	24. governor
8. last year	16. different	25. medicine

Corny jokes[2]

1. A: Jamaica?
   B: No, she came of her own accord.

2. A: Knock knock.
    B: Who's there?
    A: Jemimah.
    B: Jemimah who?
    A: Jemimah coming in? It's cold outside.

3. A: Knock knock.
    B: Who's there?
    A: Juno.
    B: Juno who?
    A: Juno your house is on fire?

The rap, 'Hello there now'

A: Hello there now,
Wher've ya bin?
I called roun'ta see ya,
Butcha never in!

B: Oh didn'tcha know
I've moved away?
I've gotta new job,
Bin gone since May.

A: Congratchalations!
That's really great.
Hey, why don'tcha
Come out an' celebrate?

B: Terrific idea!
Let's hit the town.
Dja know that new place –
The Rose 'n' Crown?

A: Yeah – see ya there
Bout half past eight.
Gotta get back now,
Don't wanna be late.

B: I've gotta go too –
It's nearly noon.
We'll have a lotta fun,
I'll see ya soon.

A&B: Bye now!

Teacher's diary

Was there any evidence that the learners became more sensitive to features of elision and assimilation by doing this activity? Did you find the jokes or the rap helped?

Notes
1. See Gillian Brown, *Listening to Spoken English* under Further reading section in the Introduction to this book.
2. See *The End*, Puffin, 1980, and *Up with Skool*, Puffin, 1981.

8 Targeting

Level	Beginner to advanced
Students	All ages
Groups	Individuals
Purpose	To give individual learners a sense of progress
Text type	As applicable to target

In this activity

Students work with the teacher to monitor chosen features of their pronunciation.

Preparation

You will need to have diagnosed some of your learners' errors in pronunciation (for a way to do this, see Appendix 1) so that you can give them realistic targets to work for. Make a 'Target check list' for each learner – the Sample teaching material is a check list for an English sound, but the form can be adapted for a stress or intonation feature too. If you have a mixed ability class, the higher level learners can be given several targets to work on at once.

Procedure

Overt method

1. Ask several individual class members to say what their target is for the lesson.

2. Provide these learners with the necessary words, phrases or larger chunks of speech which they require in order to reach their targets. They can then work on these with other learners in groups or pairs, giving and getting peer feedback.

Covert method

1. Ask the class if any of them wish to work towards a pronunciation target during the course of the lesson. Note names and targets.

2. Give a normal lesson, which may not include any work on pronunciation, but during the course of it, through monitoring small group work, or through direct student to student or teacher to student oral work, mark the 'Target check lists' for the individual students who wished to work for them.

Both methods

3. Tick the 'Target check list' as appropriate (e.g. if the student wanted to reach Target No. 5, but did not make it, tick the Target number which *was* achieved).[1]

Teacher's diary

Did you find that this activity helped learners take responsibility for their own progress? Was there any evidence of improvement over time?

Note
1. Asking learners to make a tape at intervals throughout their course will be helpful too.

Sample teaching material

Target check list

Name _____   Target sound _____

My target today is No. _____   Date _____

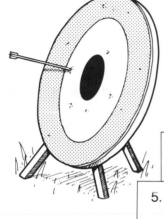

8. I can say the sound correctly whenever I need to.

7. I can say the sound correctly sometimes, in unprepared speaking.

6. I can say the sound correctly in prepared speaking.

5. I can say the sound correctly in isolated sentences.

4. I can say the sound in isolated words.

3. I can say the sound by itself.

2. I know how to pronounce the sound.

1. I can recognise the sound when others say it.

9 Dialogue completion

Level   Elementary to intermediate

Students   Teenage to adult

Groups   Pairs and individuals

Purpose   To show learners the role of pronunciation in effective
communication

Text type   Teacher's dialogues

In this activity

Students role-play a telephone dialogue, complete a one-sided dialogue, and
transcribe other students' versions of the dialogue.

Preparation

You will need an advertisement for a flat to let, and listening material on the
same topic. Make copies of the advertisement. Construct a one-sided dialogue,
which can be taken from the listening material you have chosen. Make copies
of this. Sample advertisement and dialogue are given in the Sample teaching
material section.

Procedure

1. Divide the class into pairs to role-play a telephone dialogue: one student
has advertised a flat in the newspaper, the other has seen the advertisement
and wants to rent it.

2. Hear pairs of students performing their dialogue.

3. From the students' ideas, construct a model version for the students to use
as reference. This can be written on the board for students to copy.

4. Distribute the one-sided dialogue on the same theme. Tell the students that
they should not collaborate this time, but work individually to complete the

dialogue: it is best if students can work on their dialogues orally in a language laboratory, but it can be done as a writing activity in class.

5. Now ask students to read their version onto tape, whether in the language laboratory, or as a homework task.

6. Students now swap tapes with another student, who transcribes the dialogue recorded on it. This student-to-student dictation is easy to perform in a laboratory, but you could choose a few versions to play as a whole class dictation instead.

7. Students now check their dictations both with the students whose versions they have transcribed, and with you.

8. Discuss, as a whole class, the errors and pronunciation difficulties arising from the exercise.

9. Follow up: The students will probably have had some difficulties understanding each other's accents. The supplementary material gives a set of corny jokes, and an excerpt from the popular British TV comedy show 'Allo allo!' in which the English Officer Crabtree's dreadful French accent is conveyed by his inability to get his vowels right. To follow up this activity, show the learners the jokes and see if they can say why the punchlines are funny, or show learners the comedy programme extract and see if they know how the incorrect words should be pronounced.

Sample teaching material

Advert

LONDON – NOTTING HILL: Close to tube, double room available, sharing large central flat with one other. £45 pw. Tel. to view Sat. 081–895–6540.

One-sided dialogue

A: Hello. 895–6540.

B: ....

A: Oh, yes. It's beautiful, and quite convenient for shops and the tube.

B: ....

A: I see. What kind of work do you do?

B: ....

A: Oh, well perhaps you'd like to come and have a look at it.

B: ....

A: Six o'clock suits me fine. It's at 75 Main Road. Do you know it?

B: ....

A: Fine. See you tonight then. Goodbye.

Corny jokes

1. **Teacher:** Give me a sentence with the words 'defence', 'defeat' and 'detail' in it.
   Pupil: When a horse jumps over defence, defeat go before detail!

(The substitution of /d/ for /ð/ and lack of weak vowel in the word 'the' is common in the speech of Afro-Caribbeans in England.)

2. **Child:** Please, Miss, my fumb hurts. I jammed it in the door.
   Teacher: Oh dear. Now, you mustn't say 'fumb', it's 'thumb'.
   Child: But please, Miss, my thinger hurts too.

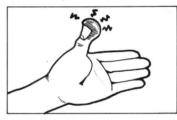

(Very young children, and some speakers from the London area, substitute /f/ for /θ/ when they speak.)

3. **Teacher:** Have you been paying attention?
   Child: Yes, Miss.
   Teacher: Well then, what is an owl?
   Child: Someone in pain, Miss.

(Many speakers 'drop their aitches' in this way.)

4. **Teacher:** Where does your Mum come from?
   Child: Alaska.
   Teacher: Don't bother, I'll ask her myself.

(In 'northern' English the vowel in 'ask' is pronounced /æ/.)

5. Did you hear about the unpopular teacher who made a spectacle of himself? His pupils were highly dilated!

(In addition to the double meaning of 'pupil' here, the pronunciation of /dɪleɪtɪd/ is also that of the word 'delighted' in what is considered to be rather upper class speech.)

6. What did the meat say when it was about to be put on the skewer? 'Spear me, oh spear me!'

(*Spear* and *spare* are homophones in some accents of English – in Scotland for example).

7. How do you get a mid-day meal in the Alps? Avalanche.

('Avalanche' is what an Italian speaker of English might say instead of 'have lunch').

TV comedy extract

Crabtree: Good <u>moaning</u>.
René: Good 'moaning'.
Crabtree: I have a <u>boon</u> to <u>peck</u> with you.
René: Oh yes?
Crabtree: Last <u>nit</u> you were supposed to send a <u>massage</u> so that the British <u>submaroon</u> could meet the <u>earmen</u>.
Edith: René, we forgot about the airmen!
Crabtree: Yes, well someone should have tipped me the <u>wonk</u>. For the last 24 <u>whores</u> they have been standing in <u>witter</u> up to their <u>nicks</u>.
Edith: René, they were in the upturned bath, in the estuary, waiting for the submarines!
René: Yes, well we are very sorry.
Crabtree: So I should <u>thonk</u>. You made me look a right <u>duckhead</u>. . . . Good <u>doo</u> to you both.

(Key: morning, bone, pick, night, message, submarine, airmen, wink, hours, water, necks, think, dickhead, day.)

Teacher's diary

Did the students find each other's accents easy to understand? Which particular difficulties arose in relating sounds to spelling?

10   'Tell me' games

Level	Beginner to advanced, depending on input
Students	Variation 1: Young adult to adult Variation 2: Children to young adult Variation 3: Children
Groups	Groups
Purpose	To improve intelligibility of pronunciation
Text type	Teacher's texts, sentences and tongue twisters

In this activity

Learners dictate to each other, using gamelike activities.

Preparation

Bring to class several short story texts, individual sentences, or tongue twisters appropriate to the class level, for variations 1, 2 and 3 respectively. The Sample teaching material gives tongue twisters.

Procedure

Any kind of dictation, in which one student dictates to another, will serve to improve pronunciation, as students have to listen carefully, then write or repeat what they have heard. The students who dictate must make a special effort to be understood, especially if their hearer is not from the same linguistic background. Here are three variations on the theme of dictation:

Variation 1: Group dictation

1. Divide the class into groups of at least three. Give out a story to each group, but the story should be divided into three parts, one part given to

each of three learners. These learners must not show their part of the text to anyone else in the group.

2. The student who has the first part of the story reads it to the rest of the group, who must all write it down. The turn then passes to the second, then the third learner, until the whole story has been written by the group as a whole.

3. Group members check their versions and make any alterations, before passing them to you for correction.

Variation 2: Team dictation

1. Divide the class into two or three equal teams. Number the team members, beginning at Number 1, and ask the team members to remember their number.

2. Your chosen tongue twisters should be written on strips of card, one tongue twister for each card. Call up the Number 1s from each team and give each person a card. The words on the card must be memorised and given back.

3. These students then go back to their teams and repeat the tongue twister to the next person in the team – the team members can confer, but only the Number 2 must go up to the teacher and repeat the tongue twister.

4. If this student is successful, then another card is issued by the teacher, memorised, and repeated to the Number 3 in the group, and so on.

5. The winning team is the first to repeat, successfully, all its tongue twisters.

    Note: If at any time a learner is unsuccessful in the attempt to recite a tongue twister to the teacher, then he or she must go back to the team for help, and try again.

Variation 3: Chinese whispers

1. Divide the class into two or three teams, and have them stand in rows.

2. Whisper a sentence to the first person in each row. This person whispers the same sentence to the next person, who whispers it to the next person, and so on down the line.

3. When the sentence reaches the last person in a line, this person rushes up to the teacher and says the sentence aloud. If it is correct, the teacher then whispers another sentence to this learner, who goes to the front of the row

this time and repeats the sentence to the first learner there, who repeats it to the next, and so on. If the sentence is incorrect, the learner must return to the end of the line, and the original learner repeats the first sentence again.

4. The game continues until every person in one team has had a turn.

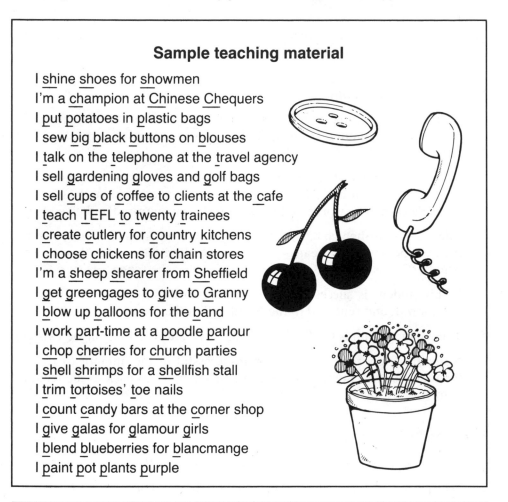

Sample teaching material

I shine shoes for showmen
I'm a champion at Chinese Chequers
I put potatoes in plastic bags
I sew big black buttons on blouses
I talk on the telephone at the travel agency
I sell gardening gloves and golf bags
I sell cups of coffee to clients at the cafe
I teach TEFL to twenty trainees
I create cutlery for country kitchens
I choose chickens for chain stores
I'm a sheep shearer from Sheffield
I get greengages to give to Granny
I blow up balloons for the band
I work part-time at a poodle parlour
I chop cherries for church parties
I shell shrimps for a shellfish stall
I trim tortoises' toe nails
I count candy bars at the corner shop
I give galas for glamour girls
I blend blueberries for blancmange
I paint pot plants purple

Teacher's diary

Which variation did you try? Was there any evidence that learners were speaking more clearly than normal?

11 Human computer[1]

Level	Beginner to advanced
Students	All ages
Groups	Individuals
Purpose	To help learners improve pronunciation of their own perceived difficulties
Text type	Teacher's reading or listening text

In this activity

Learners work on pronunciation points of their own choosing.

Preparation

None. This activity is designed to be integrated with your normal work on any reading or listening text.

Procedure

1. Work on your chosen text in the normal way. Then tell your learners that you will now act as a 'human computer' for them: you will help them pronounce any word, phrase, or whole sentence from the text which they would like to know how to say correctly. You will come and help anyone who raises his or her hand. Invite someone to begin.

2. Move to the first learner, who points to the item in the text which needs to be pronounced. Give the correct pronunciation, and let the learner repeat, as many times as the learner wants. Stop when the learner feels ready to stop – not when *you* want to.[2]

3. Repeat the process with other learners as required, for as long as time permits or until you sense that the activity has gone on long enough.

Teacher's diary

How many of the learners took advantage of the 'human computer'?
What did they choose to work on? Were they able to improve their
pronunciation?

Notes
1. The 'human computer' idea comes from a method of teaching developed by Charles
    Curran. See 'Community Language Learning' in Diane Larsen Freeman, *Techniques and
    Principles in Language Teaching*, Oxford American English, 1986, Chapter 7.
2. The rationale behind this activity is that students learn best when they have some choice in
    what they practise, and that they can take more responsibility for their own learning when
    they themselves take control of what they learn. Therefore, it is important that you do not
    evaluate what they say by saying 'Good', or 'That's right' or 'No that's not quite it'. Instead,
    let the learner be the judge of when enough practice has been done: by doing this activity
    regularly, students learn to discriminate more finely over time.

12 Read my lips

Level	Beginner to advanced
Students	All ages
Groups	Pairs
Purpose	To improve learners' articulation of English words
Text type	Teacher's word list

In this activity

Learners play a guessing game, matching their partner's lip shapes to words on a list.

Preparation

Make photocopies of a list of words containing sounds which your learners have problems pronouncing, or use the Sample teaching material for this activity, which is for a multi-lingual group and so contains many different minimal pairs.

Procedure

1. Give out copies of your word list to the students, and divide them into pairs.

2. Tell your learners to take it in turns to mouth one of the words on the list for the other learner in the pair to guess. Each learner mouths the word three times only, and the partner must tick it on the worksheet. When each learner has had six turns at mouthing a word, they then check with each other whether they have guessed correctly.

3. Tell your learners that when they have finished doing the exercise with one partner, they should find another partner to do the exercise with, using a clean worksheet. This process can be repeated with a third partner for fast finishers.

Sample teaching material

1. pig peg hid head chick cheque pit pet
2. fit pit farm palm feel peel fat pat
3. green grin bead bid meal mill feet fit
4. see she sell shell said shed save shave
5. sinner singer thin thing ban bang thick sick pass path
6. had head bag beg pan ben pack peck
7. yet jet use juice yam jam yoke joke
8. lip rip lap rap light right law raw
9. alive arrive fail pale fast past foot put
10. paper pepper pain pen age edge main men
11. low law boat bought bowl ball sew saw
12. three free thrill fill death deaf thin tin thank tank
13. mud mad fun fan butter batter drunk drank
14. pot port spot sport fox forks cot court stir star dirt dart

Teacher's diary

Which words on the list caused most problems? Were the learners able to alter their articulation to make it easier for their partner to guess?

SECTION II

WORKING WITH ENGLISH SOUNDS

Introduction

There are approximately forty-five sounds, or 'phonemes', in English, though authorities differ on the exact number and on the symbols to represent them.[1] These sounds are classified as either *vowels* or *consonants*. The vowels are often subclassified into *pure vowels* – long or short – in which the position of the lips, jaw and tongue does not change during the production of the vowel sound, and *diphthongs* (and a few *triphthongs*) in which there is a smooth glide from one sound to the next. You can see how the phonemes of English are transcribed into symbols of the International Phonetic Alphabet (I.P.A.) in Appendix 2.

English has many accents and dialects, yet it is usually possible for a native speaker to detect a 'foreign' (non-British) accent. Why is this? As far as individual sounds go, part of the reason is that, whilst English speakers tolerate a lot of variation in pronunciation, they tolerate it more in some sounds than in others. The consonants, for instance, are pronounced in a fairly uniform way across Great Britain. Moreover, one contrast which it is essential to make in English is the difference between the /s/ sound at the end of *bus* and the softer /z/ sound at the end of 'buses'. English is particularly rich in consonant 'clusters', that is where two or more consonants occur together: for example, at the beginning of *splash* and the end of *casks*. Clusters occur at the beginning, middle and end of words and often cause problems for foreign learners, who may put a vowel between the consonants, or avoid pronouncing one of them. There is a list of words containing consonant clusters in Appendix 3.

Most vowels show much more variation than is permissible in consonants, but /e/ as in *hen*, /i/ as in *seen* and /ɑ/ as in *star* do not vary much at all. There are many words in English which differ only in the contrast between /i/ and /ɪ/: for example, *meat* and *mit*, *seen* and *sin*, *beach* and *bitch*; so this is a very important contrast for foreigners to get right.[2]

One problem for learners of English is that there is no simple one-to-one relationship between a sound and the way it is represented in spelling, although there are patterns which can be taught. There is a list of possible spellings for each phoneme of English given in Appendix 4.

What we teach will ideally reflect our learners' needs, and here it should be borne in mind that far more variation is tolerated in casual conversation than in formal speech. Therefore, learners who need English for public speaking, business negotiations, or telephoning will need clear articulation; those who do not need to speak much themselves, but do have to take down in writing information given over the phone or in lectures, will require more practice in discrimination than in production; those who are aiming at near-native pronunciation will obviously need to work on finer distinctions than those who are aiming to 'get by', and so on.

There is often a mismatch between the sounds which learners can *hear* and those which they can *produce*. Discrimination practice, or ear training, is therefore a very useful first step to improving pronunciation. Activities 14, 16, 17, 18, 20, 21, 25 and 28 in this section are for discrimination practice, and do not require learners to speak.

Some teachers advocate teaching phonemic script even from very early stages of learning English. It may be useful for learners to know the symbols for phonemes which are causing them problems, in any case; Activities 15 and 19 demonstrate ways of introducing phonemic script to young learners, whilst Activity 22 can help to familiarise older learners with some of the I.P.A. symbols.

Finally, Activities 14, 24, 25, 26 and 27 are designed to improve learners' production of English sounds.

Notes
1.   See C.W. Kreidler, *The Pronunciation of English*, Blackwell, 1989, Chapter 1.
2.   Vowel quality depends on the position of the tongue, jaw and lips. For a fascinating exploration of vowel sounds in music, listen to Karlheinz Stockhausen's *Stimmung*, available from Hyperion Records Ltd, P.O. Box 25, London SE9 1AX. The score is available from Universal Edition, 2/3 Fareham Street, Dean Street, London WIV 4DU.

13 Single sound mnemonics

Level	Beginner to advanced
Students	All ages
Groups	Individuals, groups or whole class
Purpose	To introduce learners to some sounds which occur naturally in isolation
Text type	Teacher's visual mnemonics

In this activity

Students mime and say English sounds.

Preparation

The Sample teaching material for this activity is a sheet of visual mnemonics. You may like to give out copies of the visuals.

Procedure

1. Ask your learners to say if they know of any sounds which exist in English but not in their own language.

2. Tell your learners that they are going to practise some English sounds. Give out the sheet of visuals, then mime and say the sounds once through. Below is a gloss for the visuals.

    1. The sound we make every time the 'baddie' comes on stage in a play.
    2. The sound we make when we don't want other people to make a noise.
    3. The sound we make in contempt, when we don't agree.
    4. The sound we make in anticipation of a delicious meal.
    5. The sound we make for the doctor when he/she wants to look inside our mouth.
    6. The sound we make in embarrassment.

7. The sound we make in surprise – the pleasant kind.
8. The sound we make when we hesitate.
9. The sound we make to talk about ourselves.
10. The sound we make in sudden pain.
11. The sound we make when we didn't quite hear what was said.
12. The sound which means the part of the body that we hear with.
13. The sound which means the atmosphere all around us.
14. The sound we make when someone tells us an interesting piece of information.
15. The sound we make to attract attention.
16. The sound we make when we sneeze.

3. Mime and say each sound again, this time having the class repeat after you.

4. Now divide the class into groups and start a chain practice: group members sit in a circle. One learner begins with sound 1., miming as well. In a clockwise direction, the next learner round the circle gives sound 2., the next sound 3., and so on until all the sounds have been spoken and mimed. Then the learner who spoke last begins again with sound 1. and the chain is reversed around the circle, anti-clockwise this time, until all the sounds have been spoken a second time. This chain practice can be done in rows rather than circles if space is limited.

5. Finally, ask your learners if they can think of other isolated English sounds which have meaning, and/or isolated sounds in their own language – perhaps they might match the situations on the visuals?

6. Post the mnemonics around the walls of the class for correction purposes in later lessons – you can point to the visual concerned if a learner makes a mistake in pronouncing that sound.

Teacher's diary

Were the learners able to say all the sounds? Did they think of any isolated sounds which were meaningful in their own language? Could they use the pictures to correct their own pronunciation?

Sample teaching material

14   Describe and arrange

Level   Beginners

Students   All ages, but especially young learners

Groups   Variation 1: whole class; Variation 2: groups

Purpose   To improve discrimination of problem sounds
                   (Variation 1)
                   To improve discrimination and production of problem
                   sounds (Variation 2)

Text type   Teacher's word list and accompanying visuals

In this activity

Students arrange a set of pictures according to instructions.

Preparation

You will need to prepare for each student an identical set of between six and
ten picture cards illustrating problem sounds, and one for yourself. The Sample
teaching material is for problems with /θ/, /s/, /ð/ and /z/.

Procedure

Variation 1

1. Give out to each student an identical set of picture cards.

2. Shuffle your own set and place it face downwards on the desk. Then turn
    over one card at a time, without revealing it to the students, and call out
    what is on the card.

3. The students arrange their own picture cards according to the order in
    which they are turned up by the teacher.

4. The teacher then reveals the pictures to the class and checks whether students have arranged them correctly.

Variation 2

The game is played in groups, with one student per group acting as teacher.

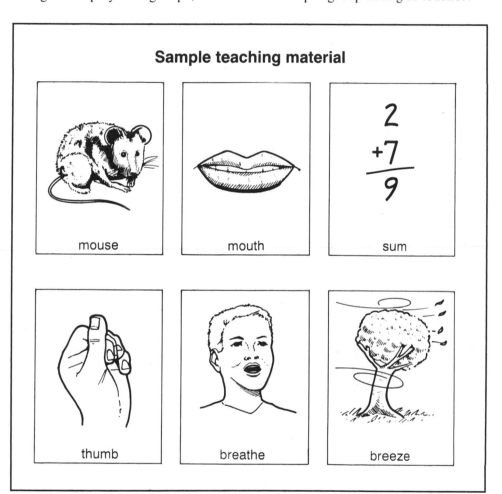

Sample teaching material

mouse

mouth

sum

thumb

breathe

breeze

Teacher's diary

Which variation did you try? What evidence did you see that the students' ability to discriminate was improved by the activity?

15 Picture — sound matching games

Level	Beginner to intermediate
Students	All ages, but especially young learners
Groups	Groups
Purpose	To improve sound discrimination. To teach some phonemic symbols.
Text type	Teacher's picture and symbol cards

In this activity

Students play a card game based on matching sounds to symbols.

Preparation

Variation 1

Pelmanism: You will need to prepare pairs of cards, one picture card matched with a corresponding phoneme card, as in the Sample teaching material. About twenty cards in all should suffice, per group. Those in the sample are chosen to practise vowel sounds.

Variation 2

Dominoes: You will need to prepare cards again, but this time they contain two images, a picture on one half and a symbol on the other, as shown in the Sample teaching material, which is chosen to practise vowel sounds.

Procedure

Variation 1

Pelmanism: *All* the cards are placed face downwards on the table, neatly in rows. The first student picks up two cards. If they form a pair, he/she keeps them. If they do not, he/she replaces them *in the same places*. The next student turns up two cards, trying to make a pair by remembering the positions of the cards already turned up, then replaced, by other students. The winner of the game is the student with most pairs, when all cards have been picked up.

Variation 2

Dominoes: The cards are shuffled and dealt equally to each player. Students take turns to lay down a card in such a way that it forms a pair with the card next to it, as in the sample sequence.

Sample teaching material

The next page gives a set of pictures which can be photocopied onto card. For Variation 1: Pelmanism, you will need to cut along each vertical and horizontal line to make small cards, some showing a single picture and some showing a single phonemic symbol, which can be matched as shown.

For Variation 2: Dominoes, you will need to cut along all the horizontal lines, but only along every other vertical line, so as to make cards containing two kinds of information, a visual and a symbol, which can be matched as shown.

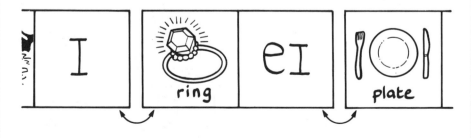

Picture – sound matching games, Sample teaching material

whale	I	ring	eɪ
plate	æ	hat	ɛ
bed	eɪ	mail	I
pin	ɛ	egg	æ
mat	aɪ	eye	u
room	ɒ	sock	aɪ
tie	u	moon	ʊ
hook	ɒ	box	eɪ

Teacher's diary

Which variation did you choose? Was there evidence that the students were learning phonemic symbols? Which sounds and symbols caused most difficulty?

16 How many sounds in the picture?

Level	Beginner to advanced
Students	All ages
Groups	Whole class, groups or pairs
Purpose	To improve sound discrimination
Text type	Teacher's picture

In this activity

Students find objects, shown in a picture, which illustrate a given sound.

Preparation

Find a suitable picture for the class to work on, or use the sample.

Procedure

Project an overhead projector transparency of your chosen picture, or give out copies of it, and ask students to find in it as many examples as they can of a given sound: for example, for the Sample teaching material, students could be asked to find /p/ sounds, and answers might include jumper, picture, lamp, pair of shoes.

Teacher's diary

Were the students able to find examples of the sound in medial or final position, as well as at the beginning of a word?

Sample teaching material

17   Classifying sounds

Level	Beginner to advanced
Students	Variations 1 and 2: young adult to adult; Variation 3: young learners
Groups	Groups or pairs
Purpose	To improve discrimination of given sounds
Text type	Teacher's word list and students' volunteered words

In this activity

Students place words in a grid or frame.

Preparation

Variation 1 and 2

You will need one copy per student of the grid or frames you wish to work with, and a list of words capable of being classified according to them.

Variation 3

Make drawings of outlines, as shown in the Sample teaching material, in which students have enough space to write appropriate words.

Procedure

Variation 1: Vowels

The Sample teaching material has been chosen with Arabic speakers in mind, and shows four vowel sounds which might be confused. Your students may confuse others, and, if so, you will need to choose four other appropriate vowel contrasts. Present your grid and chosen word list, giving one or two examples to the whole class. Then have the students work in pairs or groups to complete the grid, perhaps adding words of their own.

Variation 2: Grammar sounds

The procedure is the same as for Variation 1, but the grid may be chosen to practise classification of past tense verbs into /t/, /d/ or /ɪd/ (e.g. *watched* /t/, *saved* /d/, *needed* /ɪd/). Alternatively, the grid could be chosen to practise classification of plurals into /s/ or /z/ or /ɪz/ (e.g. *ships* /s/, *lines* /z/, churches /ɪz/).

Variation 3: Picture cards

Show one of your outlines to the class as a whole and ask them to volunteer a few words which contain the given phoneme. Then give out copies of the other frames, and have students work in pairs or groups to write in words which fit the criterion you have chosen. Finally pick a few to display around the class-room walls for reference.

Sample teaching material

Variation 1 and 2

List of words   *Classification table*

evening
picture
begin
meat
miss
friend
swam
sack
chat
spend
please
shelf

/i/	/ɪ/
ev<u>e</u>ning m<u>ea</u>t pl<u>ea</u>se	even<u>i</u>ng p<u>i</u>cture beg<u>i</u>n m<u>i</u>ss

/ɛ/	/æ/
fr<u>ie</u>nd sp<u>e</u>nd sh<u>e</u>lf	sw<u>a</u>m s<u>a</u>ck ch<u>a</u>t

Variation 3

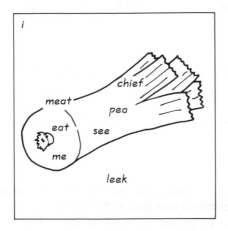

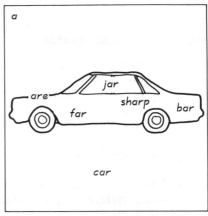

Teacher's diary

Which variation did you try? Which sounds caused problems for classification?

18 Guess my list

Level	Elementary
Students	All ages, especially young learners
Groups	Groups
Purpose	To improve discrimination and/or production of chosen phonemes. To teach recognition of phonemic symbols.
Text type	Teacher's picture set

In this activity

Students play a game which involves them in selecting items with given phonemes.

Preparation

For each group of three to four students, you will need a picture set of items which might be bought at a supermarket (about 20 items in all).

Procedure

1. Divide the class into groups, or teams. If you have a multi-lingual class it may be interesting to divide them according to first language, since each group will then have common pronunciation problems which you can target.

2. Give each group of students a copy of your chosen picture set.

3. Then give each group a 'sound' to work with, preferably by giving them a piece of paper on which you have written its phonemic symbol. The task is for each group to find the items in the picture set which contain their 'sound'.

4. When the groups have finished, check their answers. The winning group is the one with most correct items.

Sample teaching material

You might include a picture of *bread*, *birthday card* and *saucepan*. If one group is working with /θ/, they will include *birthday card* but neither of the other two, whilst a group working with /d/ can include both *bread* and *birthday card*, but not *saucepan*.

Teacher's diary

Were you able to target particular difficulties? Did you see any evidence that discrimination was being improved?

19 Phonemic script team game

Level	Elementary to intermediate
Students	Young learners
Groups	Groups
Purpose	To familiarise learners with phonemic symbols
Text type	Teacher's list of phonemes and corresponding symbols

In this activity

Students play a team game involving recognition of phonemic symbols

Preparation

Decide which and how many phonemic symbols you wish to work with, and be prepared to write them on the board.

Procedure

1. Write a number of phonemic symbols in random order on the board.

2. Divide the class into two equal teams, each member of which is given a number.

3. Call out a sound corresponding to one of the symbols on the board, then call out a number. For example, if you call out '/t/, one', then the *first* member of each team comes to the board and circles the correct symbol. The first person to do so scores a point for his/her team.

4. Continue in the same way for as long as you like – it does not matter how many times a given phoneme is called, so long as you erase the circles each time they are drawn by team members.

Variation

Instead of individual phonemes, you could write a random list of words, or a random list of phonemic transcriptions of these words, as a basis for the same game.

Teacher's diary

Were individual class members able to carry out the task? Were some quicker than others, so that this activity helped diagnose weaknesses?

20 Odd sound out

Level   Beginner to advanced

Students   Young adult to adult

Groups   Whole class, pairs or groups

Purpose   To improve sound discrimination

Text type   Teacher's word list

In this activity

Students circle the 'odd one out' in given word lists.

Preparation

Make one copy of your chosen word sets per student, or per pair of students. (An example word set is given in the Sample teaching material.) Each set should contain four words, three containing a given sound, and one 'odd one out'.

Procedure

1. Give out copies of your chosen word sets and have students work alone, in pairs, or in groups to circle the word which does not fit the pattern.

2. Have groups of learners compare their answers with others before giving whole class feedback.

Sample teaching material

In the set: water, daughter, laughter, mortar, the word *laughter* is the odd sound out, the other three having the phoneme /ɔ/, which is missing in *laughter*.

Teacher's diary

How easy or difficult was this activity for your learners? Did the activity improve awareness of sound-spelling relationships?

21 Sound puzzles

Level   Elementary to advanced

Students   All ages, especially teenagers

Groups   Whole class, pairs or groups

Purpose   To improve sound-spelling awareness

Text type   Teacher's crossword puzzle or wordsearch

In this activity

Students complete a crossword grid or wordsearch.

Preparation

Prepare a crossword or wordsearch for which every answer has a given sound. In the Sample teaching material, the common sound is /ɜ/.

Procedure

Project an overhead projector transparency of your chosen puzzle, or distribute copies of it. Give students time to work alone, in pairs, or groups to complete it, then check their answers with others, before you provide the correct answers.

Teacher's diary

Were the students able to identify the target sound? Was there evidence that the activity helped the students' ability to discriminate?

Sample teaching material

Wordsearch

Every answer has the sound /ɜ/. Find words which mean the following:

- the opposite of late
- something that flies
- a place where people go to pray
- the day after Wednesday
- something that men wear
- when you put something in the fire, it _____
- first, second, _____

t	u	r	i	z	o	b
y	h	a	b	g	y	h
n	o	i	i	l	t	c
c	h	u	r	c	h	a
t	r	a	d	d	u	f
m	e	s	h	i	r	t
t	b	u	r	n	s	e
h	a	d	y	o	d	i
s	i	g	r	d	a	s
o	v	n	s	i	y	t

22 Phonemic scrabble[1]

Level   Advanced

Students   Adults

Groups   Groups

Purpose   To improve students' knowledge of phonemic script

Text type   Phonemic scrabble board and tiles or cards

In this activity

Students play a board game to aid memorisation of phonemic symbols.

Preparation

The equipment you will need is a square-shaped board divided into about 20 × 20 small squares, and a pool of phoneme tiles or cards which fit the squares. You will need one set for each group. The Sample teaching material gives the symbols you need, and a frequency chart. Photocopy the symbols onto card, making more cards for the frequent phonemes than you do for the infrequent ones.

Procedure

1. Divide the class into groups and give each group a game board and set of tiles or cards. A list of phonemic symbols will also be useful (see Appendix 2).

2. Demonstrate the game with one group: Put all the phoneme tiles/cards face downwards on the table, and tell each member of the group to take a given number, unseen (seven tiles seems about right). The first player looks at his/her phonemes and tries to make an English word in sound (e.g. /si/ for 'see'). If he/she can do so, he/she lays down this word on the game board. The next player looks at his/her phonemes and does the same, making the word fit in crossword fashion, as in the Sample teaching material for /min/

(mean). The game continues in this way. If players cannot make a word, they pick up another tile/card from the pool.

3. Have the groups begin the game simultaneously.

4. After a given time, say twenty minutes, players count one point for each tile/card left in their hand. The player with the smallest number wins. Make sure you check the boards to see whether the words are all correct transcriptions of English sounds before declaring the winner.

Sample teaching material

Game board

A typical game board might look like the one below.

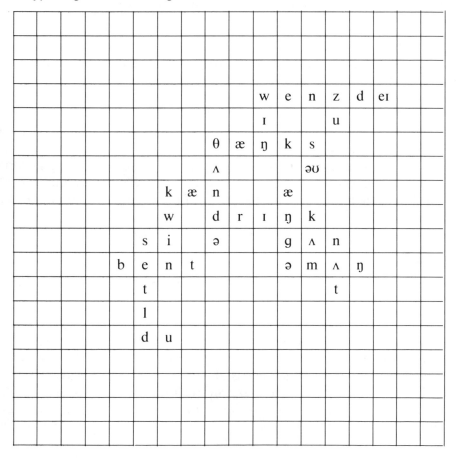

Phonemic symbols

f	p	h	ŋ	g
ʃ	ə	ɛ	aɪ	ʌ
eɪ	i	n	t	d
s	l	ð	v	b
ɔɪ	ʊə	u	ʊ	j
wild consonant	dʒ	ʒ	θ	tʃ
wild vowel	I	əʊ	æ	ɒ
	ɔ	r	m	k
	w	z	ɑ	aʊ
	ɜ	ɛə	ɪə	

Chart of frequencies of English phonemes[2]

Vowels			**Consonants**	
Phoneme	*Frequency*		*Phoneme*	*Frequency*
/ə/	10.74%		/n/	7.58%
/ɪ/	8.33%		/t/	6.42%
/ɛ/	2.97%		/d/	5.14%
/aɪ/	1.83%		/s/	4.81%
/ʌ/	1.75%		/l/	3.66%
/eɪ/	1.71%		/ð/	3.56%
/i/	1.65%		/r/	3.51%
/əʊ/	1.51%		/m/	3.22%
/æ/	1.45%		/k/	3.09%
/ɒ/	1.37%		/w/	2.81%
/ɔ/	1.24%		/z/	2.46%
/u/	1.13%		/v/	2.00%
/ʊ/	0.86%		/b/	1.97%
/ɑ/	0.79%		/f/	1.79%
/aʊ/	0.61%		/p/	1.78%
/ɜ/	0.52%		/h/	1.40%
/ɛə/	0.34%		/ŋ/	1.15%
/ɪə/	0.21%		/g/	1.05%
/ɔɪ/	0.14%		/ʃ/	0.88%
/ʊə/	0.06%		/j/	0.88%
			/dʒ/	0.60%
			/tʃ/	0.41%
			/θ/	0.37%
			/ʒ/	0.10%

Teacher's diary

How well were the students able to 'spell' English words phonemically? Did their ability to do this improve during the activity? Which phonemes caused most difficulty?

Notes
1. I am indebted to Chris Jones of Naples University for the idea of using 'Scrabble' for teaching phonemic script.
2. See A.C. Gimson, *An Introduction to the Pronunciation of English*, Arnold, 1980 (3rd edn).

23 Sound ladders

Level	Beginner to advanced
Students	Young learners
Groups	Individuals
Purpose	To improve articulation and speed of articulation of a given sound
Text type	Individual problem sounds

In this activity

Students connect visuals or movements with sounds.

Preparation

None, but prior diagnosis of students' difficulties with pronunciation will need to have been made, so that you direct each learner to work on the sound(s) he/she needs to practise. (For a tool of diagnosis, see Appendix 1.)

Procedure

Draw a picture of a ladder on the board. It should have at least ten rungs. Then have individual learners say their problem sound(s) as many times as they can – each utterance of the sound corresponds to one rung of the ladder. If they manage to reach the top, then time them to see how quickly they can do so.

Variation

Draw the ladder on the floor with chalk and have learners physically step up a rung each time they say the sound(s).

Teacher's diary

Did the visual representation help articulation? Try the same technique using a word containing the sound and see if it works as well.

24 Memory game

Level	Beginner to advanced
Students	All ages
Groups	Whole class or groups
Purpose	To improve production of problem sounds
Text type	Student generated

In this activity

Students play a memory game which increases in difficulty the longer it goes on.

Preparation

You will need to base this on the pronunciation difficulties which you have diagnosed. (For diagnosis, see Appendix 1.) From this, prepare a phoneme card or cards for each learner. For example, /l/ and /r/ for Japanese students, /b/ and /v/ for Spanish students.

Procedure

1. Distribute the phoneme cards – if your students are unfamiliar with phonemic script, just use normal English spelling of a sample word, with the sound you want to target underlined.

2. Begin the game yourself with the sentence: 'I went to the supermarket and I bought an apple'. The next person continues by repeating what you have said, and adding another item which includes that person's problem sound (e.g. 'a lemon' or 'an umbrella' for a Japanese student, 'a vanilla ice cream' for a Spanish student). The next player repeats the original sentence, adds what the second player said, and adds his/her own item to the list.

3. The game continues until somebody forgets an item, or after an agreed time limit.

Variation

For younger or lower level learners, you might like to provide each learner with a list of possible items having their problem sound, from which they can choose an item to add to the list, when it is their turn to speak.

Teacher's diary

Did you find that the game format helped learners to produce their problem sounds? Can you think of other memory games which you could adapt for work on pronunciation?

---

25 Sounds travel game[1]

Level	Intermediate
Students	Teenage to adult
Groups	Groups
Purpose	To familiarise learners with the pronunciation of place names
Text type	Names of towns

In this activity

Students play a travel game based on a map of Great Britain – or whichever English speaking country the students need to be most familiar with.

Preparation

You will need to make one copy per group of a map of your chosen English speaking country, showing well known towns or tourist spots. Decide which English sounds you want your learners to work with, or use the ones from the Sample teaching material.

Procedure

1. Tell your students that they are going to plan a tourist visit, of two weeks, and they have to choose an itinerary which includes only place names having a particular sound – they will be given this by the teacher. They must include a given number of places (ten is about right). For lower levels a list of places, from which they choose, can be provided, as in the Sample teaching material.

2. Distribute the maps (one per group) and the sound you have chosen. Each group can have the same sound, or different ones.

3. Set a time limit for the task, and tell the groups to begin planning their route.

4. When the time is up, ask each group to explain their route to the others, and check that all the places they have chosen include the given sound.

Variation

With more advanced learners, groups could guess each others' sound from their itineraries. Alternatively, they could question each other to find out the sound (e.g. Are you going to visit Stonehenge? – Yes – What about Harrogate? – Yes – Is your sound /h/? – Yes).

Sample teaching material

Higher levels

Students choose their own itineraries. Examples are:

For Southern Ireland, target sound /k/: Kildare, Kirkwall, Kilkenny, Carlow, Kilkee, Carrick Fergus, Enniskillen, Kilkooly Abbey, Limerick (but not Knock, etc.)

For Scotland, target sound /w/: Kirkwall, Wideford Hill, Cuween, Whiten Head, Lerwick, Weem, Fowlis Wester, Fort William, North Uist, Winton House (but not Berwick, Bowden Hill, etc.)

For England, target sound /h/: Heveningham Hall, Market Harborough, Haddon Hall, Huddersfield, Birkenhead, Hemel Hempstead, High Wycombe, Wookey Hole Caves, Hastings, Honiton (but not Norwich, Burgh Castle, Brighton, etc.)

Lower levels

Students can be given a complete itinerary, which they mark on the map, then choose only the places having their target sound; for example:

For target sounds /r/, /k/, /θ/, /tʃ/

Complete itinerary: Sunderland, Middlesbrough, Darlington, Lancaster, Preston, Blackburn, Liverpool, Manchester, Sheffield, Nottingham, Leicester, Birmingham, Cheltenham, Portsmouth, Hertford, Chelmsford, Cambridge, Ipswich, Worthing, Southend, etc.

From this itinerary, the /r/ group could choose Middlesbrough and Preston but not Sunderland or Liverpool; the /k/ group could choose Lancaster as well as Cambridge; the /θ/ group could choose Southend but not Worthing; the /tʃ/ group could choose Chelmsford and Cheltenham but not Sheffield.

Teacher's diary

Did the learners enjoy the activity? What evidence was there that their knowledge of the pronunciation of the place names had improved? Can you think of other ways of using place names for pronunciation work?

Note
1. This game would be a good warm-up activity for work on the topic of travel and tourism, as well as one way of making learners familiar with the geography of the country they are visiting/likely to visit.

26 Information gap shopping list

Level	Elementary to advanced, depending on input
Students	All ages
Groups	Pairs
Purpose	To improve production of problem sounds
Text type	Teacher's paired shopping lists

In this activity

Students ask each other for information whilst practising problem sounds.

Preparation

You will need to prepare pair work material, as in the Sample teaching material, enough for the class to work in simultaneous pairs.

Procedure

1. Arrange the seating so that pairs of students can work together without seeing each other's material. This can be done either by having a piece of folded card acting as a screen between students, or by having the students sit back to back.

2. Tell the students that they must complete their grids by asking each other for information; for example, in the sample, Student A asks, 'How many elastic bands have we got?' and Student B is able to give the information.

Variations

There are many other situations which can be used as a basis for similar activity, in which one member of the pair has a list of items to be bought or found, and the other has helpful information; for example, one student could have a list of ingredients for a recipe, and the other could have an inventory of foodstuffs already in the kitchen cupboards.

Sample teaching material

Student A's card: (Target sound /l/)

Rubric: You and your partner have been asked to carry out a stock check on the following items: elastic bands, black ball point pens, typewriter ribbons, drawing pins, blue ball point pens, and A4 envelopes. Work together to give the required information to your boss,* when he/she comes into the office.

Item	Quantity
elastic bands	
typewriter ribbons	25
black ball point pens	
drawing pins	6 boxes
A4 envelopes	
blue ball point pens	?150

Student B's card: (Target sound /p/ and /b/)

Same rubric as on A's card, but different information as shown below.

Item	Quantity
elastic bands	1 box
typewriter ribbons	
black ball point pens	50
drawing pins	
A4 envelopes	100
blue ball point pens	?100

* The role of the boss can be taken by the teacher or by another student.

Teacher's diary

What evidence did you find that learners were able to use their target sound in context? Can you think of other situations which can be used for this activity?

---

27 Can I come to the party?

Level	Intermediate
Students	All ages
Groups	Whole class
Purpose	To improve learners' production of problem sounds in connected speech
Text type	Teacher's tongue twisters

In this activity

Students play a communication game involving tongue twisters.

Preparation

You will need to prepare a tongue twister for each student. Write each one on a separate strip of paper. The tongue twisters should refer to a type of employment (see Sample teaching material for Activity 10 for a list of such tongue twisters). If possible, match problem sounds to individual students. (For diagnostic methods see Appendix 1.) The target sound should always come at the *beginning* of a word.

Procedure

1. Give each student the tongue twister you have prepared. Each student must memorise the tongue twister, without revealing it to anyone else, and then give back the paper to you.

2. Tell the students that they are to find other students to go to a party with them. They can only go together if their jobs involve identical sounds. Use the Sample teaching material below to demonstrate how the game proceeds. Set a time limit for the task – say, ten minutes.

3. Tell the students to begin the game. They should mill about the classroom asking as many students as they can, within the allotted time.

4. When time is up, ask the students to form into groups of people who can go to the party together, and ask them to say what they do.

Sample teaching material

A full list of tongue twisters is given in the Sample teaching material for Activity 10.

A: (Target sound /p/) Hello. What do you do?

B: (Target sound /p/) I paint pictures of poodles.

A: Oh, do you really? Then you can come to the party with me. I print papers for the Patching Group. Let's ask Mary. Hello, Mary. What's your job?

C: (Target sound /s/) I serve sausages at the supermarket.

B: Oh dear, I'm afraid you can't come with us then.

Teacher's diary

Were the students able to understand each others' accents? Did their pronunciation improve during the activity?

28 The yes/no game

Level　　　　Beginner to advanced

Students　　All ages, especially young learners

Groups　　　Whole class

Purpose　　　To improve discrimination of consonant sounds

Text type　　Teacher's word list

In this activity

Students play an elimination game based on sound discrimination.

Preparation

Prepare a list of words containing consonants which cause difficulty for your learners (see Appendix 8). The Sample teaching material below has been chosen with Spanish speakers in mind, and involves contrasts between /n/ and /ŋ/, /s/ and /θ/. For each student, make two cards, one marked YES and the other marked NO. If you can make all the YES cards one colour and the NO cards another, this will make things easier for you during the game.

Procedure

1. Give each learner a YES card and a NO card.

2. Explain that the learners will hear a list of words, some of which will contain a given sound. After each word, they must hold up one of their cards – YES if they think the word contains the given sound, and NO if not. If a learner holds up the wrong card, he/she is out of the game, and so is the last learner to raise a card.

3. Begin the game. It need not be based on one target sound alone, but on several, as in the sample. The game ends when only one learner is left in.

Sample teaching material

Word list: singer   rang   ran   thing   thin   sin
Teacher instruction: Hold up a YES card if you think you hear /n/ (or /θ/). Hold up your NO card if you don't hear the sound.

Teacher's diary

Was there any evidence that this activity improved your learners' ability to discriminate? Which sound(s) caused most problems?

SECTION III

WORKING WITH ENGLISH RHYME AND RHYTHM

Introduction

In studies of how we acquire our native language, it has been shown[1] that there is a strong relationship between early knowledge of rhyme and subsequent success in reading and spelling. Many teachers of native-speaking English children, when teaching writing, introduce children to rhyme as a first step in handling phonic analysis and synthesis. There is considerable evidence that children's sensitivity to rhyme and alliteration, gained through nursery rhymes, provides a pathway through to awareness of the component sounds in words. In teaching English as a foreign language, we can take account of these findings and allow our learners to hear, learn, recite and make recordings of appropriate rhymes and jingles. Activities 29, 30, 31, 32, 33 and 37 are designed to foster awareness of rhyme in English.

Our strongest memories are often linked with strong emotions, which, in turn, are affected by information we take in through our senses. Poetry appeals to the emotions, and thereby facilitates memorisation of new information. Just listening to the way the language is spoken, to the sounds which occur together, to whether they seem 'harsh' or 'soft', 'stimulating' or 'relaxing' can be a useful activity for learners. Often we may be too quick to launch into an exploration of the *message* of a poem, without allowing time for appreciation of its *sound*. Of course, learners can be asked to repeat and recite, but some may prefer just to listen. Action rhymes, such as those in Activity 34, are appropriate for young and elementary learners because actions have to be synchronised with the strong beats of the internal rhythm. Rapping can be used for older and more sophisticated learners, who can clap, click fingers or tap toes to the strong beats, as in Activity 35. At advanced level, especially, poetry gives us a legitimate opportunity to talk about language and to analyse it, as in Activities 29, 36 and 37.

Like movement and colour, melody is thought to be encoded in the right side of the brain, so that if we link the words we want to teach with music, they should be better remembered than by using the purely verbal, left side of the brain. For centuries, teachers have used choral repetition or chanting, songs and action songs (words with music and movement) because they knew these techniques were effective. Current neurolinguistic research has validated these tried and tested methods.[2] For evidence of the power of melody to 'fix' words in the memory, you have only to recall the tune of your favourite song, and you will remember the words along with it. These days, popular songs have a great influence, especially on young people, and, since they are mostly sung in English, why not use them to teach the rhythm of English? Activity 34 uses songs as a basis for work on rhythm.

Teachers who wish to improve the rhythm of their learners' English are faced with the problem of understanding the nature of stress itself. Stress is commonly thought to have three parameters – pitch, length, and loudness.[3] Pitch has been found to be by far the most efficient indicator of main stress. This kind of stress will be dealt with in Part IV of this book. The parameters of length and loudness have not been shown to be very good indicators of stress. Roach[4] records that, in his experiments, native speakers, of various languages, found it 'an impossibly difficult task' to say which syllables were stressed in recordings of their own speech. One thing we *can* say, however, is that syllable quantities in English really do vary, largely because of our 'full vowels' and 'weak vowels'.[5] Consider the italicised vowels in '*a*bout', 'sill*i*ness' and 'nar-rower', all of which are unstressed. Now consider the phrase 'an unforgettable lesson'. If we mark the syllables as 'weak' (W) or 'full' (F), we come up with the pattern:

an un-for-get-ta-ble les-son
W F W F W W   F W

It is the alternation of full and reduced vowels which determines English syllable quantities and gives English its characteristic rhythm. Appendix 5 gives a list of weak forms and Activity 38 practises them.

EFL teachers who want their students to speak an English which will be easily understood by a native speaker will need to concentrate on helping them to produce a) correctly reduced vowels and b) correct 'stress placement'. Many learners are used to invariable stress placement in their own language and find our movable stress (e.g. in *pho*tograph, pho*to*grapher) difficult to cope with. Prefixes and suffixes play a part in our rules for stress placement, and some of these are practised in Activities 40 and 41. Appendix 6 gives some stress rules also. Movable stress is the subject of Activities 39, 40, 41 and 42, but is treated more fully in Section IV.

Notes

1. See B.E. Bryant, L. Bradley, M. McLean, J. Crossland, 'Nursery Rhymes, phonological skills and reading' in *Journal of Child Language*, 16 (1989), pp. 407–428.
   See also I. Lundberg, J. Frost, O. Petersen, 'Effects of an extensive program for stimulating phonological awareness in preschool children' in *Reading Research Quarterly*, Vol. XXIII/3 (Summer 1988), pp. 263–284.

2. See G. Lozanov, 'Suggestology and Suggestopedy' in R. Blair, *Innovative Approaches to Language Teaching*, Rowley, 1982.
   See also *L'eveil et l'harmonie de l'enfant*, available from the French Research on Yoga in Education group, College Condorcet, Rue d'Amsterdam, 75008 Paris.
   See also Barbara Meister Vitale, *Free Flight*, Salmar Press, 1986.

3. For further activities using songs, see *Songs in Action*.

4. The references to pitch, length and loudness are made in Roach 1991 (see Further reading in the Introduction to this book). See also D. Faber, 'Teaching the Rhythms of English, a new theoretical base' in IRAL, 24 (1986), pp. 205–216.

5. D. Faber, op. cit.

29 The cat sat on the mat

Level	Intermediate to advanced
Students	All ages
Groups	Whole class, pairs or groups
Purpose	To raise learners' awareness of rhyme
Text type	Teacher's rhyming words

In this activity

Students volunteer rhyming words.

Preparation

Bring to class several examples of words capable of generating many rhymes. If possible, also bring along poems or jingles which demonstrate the rhymes in action.

Procedure

1. Give an example of some rhyming words (e.g. sat, mat, cat, fat) and ask your students for more rhymes. The list generated can be written on the board.

2. Divide the class into groups or pairs and give each a word. All the groups/pairs can be given the same word, or different ones. Tell them that their task is to produce as many rhymes as they can for the word, within an allotted time limit.

3. After the allotted time, bring the class together to report back on their rhymes, and check the accuracy of what they have produced.

4. Give out copies of your chosen poems/jingles as authentic evidence of the rhymes in action.

5. Depending on their level, students can be asked to compose a poem of their own using the rhymes. (They could even be set to music.)

Sample teaching material[1]

A really hot meal

A really hot meal
Doesn't appeal
To a Seal.
Its favourite dish
Is very cold fish!

Gavin Ewart

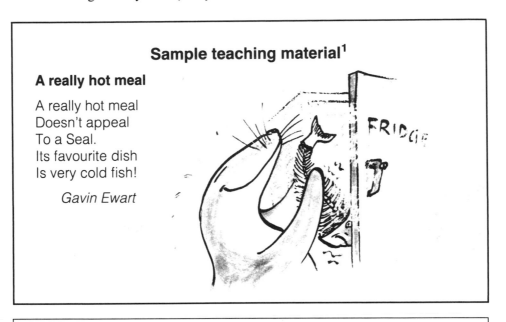

Teacher's diary

How easy was it for the students to carry out this activity? Was there evidence that they had become more sensitive to rhyme through doing it?

Note
1. From *A Catalogue of Comic Verse*, compiled by Rolf Harris for Knight Books, 1988.

30   Rhyme sets/rhyme pairs

Level	Elementary to intermediate
Students	All ages, especially young learners
Groups	Whole class or groups
Purpose	To raise awareness of rhyme
Text type	Teacher's set of rhyming object pictures

In this activity

Students compete to find a number of rhyming objects.

Preparation

Bring to class copies of worksheets showing pictures of rhyming objects, as in the Sample teaching material.

Procedure

1. Divide the class into groups and give each group a copy of your worksheet.

2. Tell the groups that their task is to find pairs of objects which rhyme, and to write down the names of the objects, set out in their pairs.

3. Set a time limit for the task, and tell the groups to begin.

4. When the time is up, bring the class together to report on their findings. The winning group is the one with most rhymes correct.

Variation

Instead of matching *pairs* of rhyming objects, students can be asked to find *sets* of rhyming objects. This is a more difficult task, and it can be made more difficult still if you do not specify how many rhyming objects there are in each set.

Sample teaching material

The name of each object rhymes with another object. Can you find the rhyming words?

Key

lock – cock
dog – log
pail – nail
fork – cork

Teacher's diary

How easy was this activity for the students? Did they use their dictionaries for pronunciation information?

31 Rhyming work cards

Level	Elementary to intermediate
Students	All ages, especially young learners
Groups	Whole class, pairs or groups
Purpose	To help learners' mastery of spelling, using rhyme as an aid
Text type	Teacher's work cards

In this activity

Students complete sets of rhyming words.

Preparation

You will need to make work cards showing a picture of the target rhyme at the top, with blank spaces for rhyming words below, the initial consonant of which is given. A sample card is given in the Sample teaching material.

Procedure

1. Divide the class into groups or pairs and give each some work cards to complete. (For a competitive game, each group or pair can have the same set of work cards. For a workshop-type activity, they can be given different ones.)

2. Set a time limit for the task, and tell the students to begin work.

3. After the allotted time, bring the class together to check answers. The group or pair with most completed work cards, correct of course, wins.

4. Follow up: Students could be given a rhyme, rap or song in which some of the rhymes have been blanked out, and they could try to fill each blank with a plausible rhyme.

Sample teaching material

Example: GATE

f _____

a _____

w _____

gr _____

b _____

Teacher's diary

Did you find much variation in the students' ability to spell? Was this improved by the activity?

32 Rhyming snap

Level	Beginners to advanced, depending on input
Students	All ages
Groups	Groups
Purpose	To raise awareness of rhyme
Text type	Teacher's rhyme cards

In this activity

Students play a card game involving matching rhymes.

Preparation

You will need to prepare word cards for learners to play with in groups of four. Four to six rhyming words, for six to ten sounds, will be needed. For elementary learners, these could be very simple (e.g. BAKE, MAKE, WAKE, FLAKE), but more complex rhymes can be used at intermediate level, for which the Sample teaching material is designed.

Procedure

1. Divide the class into groups and give each group a set of cards.

2. Tell one person in each group to deal the cards equally amongst the group. Players should not look at the cards, but keep them face downwards in a pile, exactly as dealt.

3. The first player turns up the first card on his/her pile and places it face up in the middle of the table. The next player does the same. If it makes a pair with the preceding card, by rhyming with it, the player keeps the pair. If not, the turn passes to the next player, who places another card on top of the last one. The game continues until all the cards have been played. Players then count up how many pairs they have made. The winner is the player with most pairs.

4. At the end of the game, check that each group's pairs are correct.

Sample teaching material

SOW	KNEE	ALLOW	ROUGH	BELOW
TRAY	DENY	SEA	GREY	NEW
EYE	LIE	OBEY	SHE	LEIGH
MAY	SUE	TIE	HIGH	GO
PLAY	SEW	NEIGH	FLEA	ROW
APPLY	ENOUGH	FEW	PURVEY	CUE
SKY	WHY	BOW	SLEIGH	BOUGH
OWE	TOE	WEIGH	WHEY	NOW
COUGH	KNOW	ROUGH	CUFF	OFF

Teacher's diary

Did the activity give rise to discussion about possible ways of pronouncing the words on the cards? Was there any evidence that the game was helping to improve learners' awareness of spelling rules?

33 Colour rhyme bingo

Level	Elementary to advanced, depending on input
Students	All ages
Groups	Groups
Purpose	To improve learners' knowledge of rhyme and of sound-spelling relationships
Text type	Teacher's card game

In this activity

Students play a matching game involving colour association and rhyming words.

Preparation

You will need a colour die – you can buy one[1]; or make one by painting each of the six faces of a small cube in a different colour; or use a hexagon of stiff card, each side coloured differently, with a pencil pushed through the centre to make a spinner. For six players, you will need a die, six Bingo cards, and thirty-six word cards. The Sample teaching material gives all you need for practising the vowel sounds /i/, /eɪ/, /aɪ/, /ɔ/, /əʊ/ and /ɒ/. You can adapt it for practising other vowel combinations.

Procedure

1. Write on the board the six words from the Bingo card you will use for the game.

2. Ask your students to volunteer words which can rhyme with the words you have written on the board. Give them examples for the first word (e.g. for eat: meat, treat, etc.).

3. Tell the learners that they are going to play a game with rhyming words. Divide the class into groups of six and choose one group to demonstrate the game, inviting other students to come and watch.

4. Demonstrate the game as follows:
    Give each member of the group a Bingo card. This shows six 'bricks', each brick coloured to correspond with the colours on your die. These bricks show the target rhymes. Next, shuffle the word cards, which are cut to exactly the size of the bricks, and place them face down in the middle of the table. The first player throws the die and picks up a word card. If the word on the card rhymes with the relevant brick on the Bingo card, the player covers the brick with the word card; for example, if the player throws 'green' and picks up the word card 'meet', he looks at the Bingo card to see if the green brick rhymes with 'meet'. If it does, the brick can be covered; if not, the word card is replaced at the bottom of the pile and the turn passes to the next player. The game continues until one of the players has covered all six of his/her bricks.

5. Set the groups to work simultaneously with their set of the game. Monitor the groups, giving advice where needed, and taking note of any difficulties. Set a time limit for the game.

6. After the allotted time, bring the class together for feedback, writing on the board any words which caused confusion, and practising pronunciation.

Sample teaching material

Bingo card to practise sounds /i/, /eɪ/, /aɪ/, /ɔ/, /əʊ/, /ɒ/.
Colour key: eat = green, hate = red, might = yellow,
nought = blue, coat = white, cot = pink.

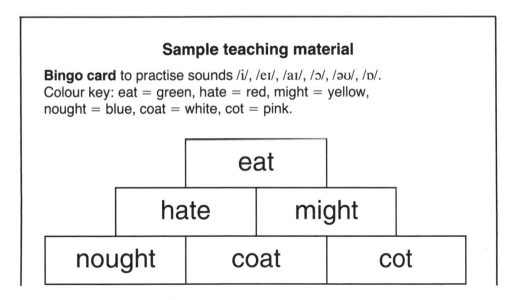

Word cards (36 minimum)

e.g.

spot	plot	watt	what	lot	date
meet	plate	note	stoat	wart	bought
write	sleet	mate	caught	throat	great
fort	bite	wheat	late	beat	site
wrote	boat	height	receipt	great	rote
wait	night	quart	knot	seat	light

Teacher's diary

How easy was it for the learners to play the game? Did the group members help each other with pronunciation whilst playing? Were you able to make any new diagnosis of errors by doing this activity with the class?

Note
1. Winslow Press, Telford Road, Bicester, Oxon, OX6 0TS and Taskmaster Ltd, Morris Road, Leicester, LE2 6BR are two producers of teaching resources of a practical nature, and especially of spelling and pronunciation aids.

34 Action rhymes

Level	Elementary
Students	Young learners
Groups	Whole class
Purpose	To help learners develop a sensitivity to English rhythm by synchronising actions with strong stresses
Text type	Teacher's rhymes

In this activity

Students recite rhymes whilst performing related actions.

Preparation

Use the rhymes and actions in the Sample teaching material, or devise your own actions to accompany your chosen rhymes.

Procedure

1. Invite your learners to form a circle, or, if this is not possible, to stand where they are.

2. Say the rhyme yourself, with the accompanying actions.

3. Say each line, with learners repeating after you and copying your actions. You may need to explain necessary vocabulary (e.g. *plum* and *wave* in the Sample teaching material) by drawing on the board to make meaning clear.

4. Say the whole rhyme, slowly, with the class performing the actions together.

5. If space permits, and you are in a circle, invite pairs of learners to stand in the middle of the circle and recite the rhyme together, with the actions, whilst the rest of you walk slowly around them.

Variation

Action songs: The procedure is the same as above, but you will need to sing the rhyme instead of just speaking it. The action songs in the Sample teaching material are designed to teach parts of the body, and the music is provided, along with the actions.

Sample teaching material[1]

Rhymes

1. Three red plums
(Traditional)

Rhyme	Action
Three red plums on the	Put up three fingers
old plum tree	Lift arms above head and down again to make the shape of a tree with branches
One for you and	Point to another person
one for me and	Point to self
one for the boy who	Point to another person
picks them	Make picking movement with fingers of both hands

Rhythm in musical notation

Three red plums on the   old plum tree   One for you and   one for me and

one for the boy who   picks   them

2. There are big waves
(Eleanor Farjeon)

Rhyme	*Action*
There are <u>big</u> waves and	*Reach up high*
<u>little</u> waves,	*Reach down low*
<u>Green</u> waves and <u>blue</u>.	*Make wave motion with hands*
<u>Waves</u> you can <u>jump</u> over,	*Jump on the word 'jump'*
<u>Waves</u> you <u>dive through</u>.	*Put hands together and make diving motion*
<u>Waves</u> that rise <u>up</u> like a	*Reach up high with both hands*
<u>great</u> water <u>wall</u>.	*and stand on tiptoes*
<u>Waves</u> that swell <u>softly</u> and	*Put finger on lips to signal 'quiet'*
<u>don't</u> break at <u>all</u>.	*Shake head to signal 'no'*
<u>Waves</u> that can <u>whisper</u>.	*Say this line very softly*
<u>Waves</u> that can <u>roar</u>.	*Say this line loudly*
<u>Tiny</u> waves that <u>run</u> at you,	*Run forward with little steps*
<u>Running</u> on the <u>shore</u>	*Run backwards slowly on tiptoes*

Rhythm in musical notation

Action songs

1. Head and shoulders

Song	*Action*
Head and shoulders, knees	*Touch each part of the body*
and toes, knees and toes	*mentioned, each time you say its name*
(Repeat)	
and eyes and ears and	
mouth and nose,	
Head and shoulders, knees	
and toes, knees and toes.	

Now repeat the whole song but this time don't sing the word *head*, just touch it, each time it comes up in the song.

Now sing the whole song a third time, but don't sing *head* or *shoulders*, just touch them, and so on.

Continue in the same way, leaving out the word for each succeeding part of the body, but performing the action. You will reach a point where you are singing only the word 'and'.

_____ and _____, _____ and _____, _____ and _____, _____ and _____, _____ and _____, _____ and _____ and _____ and _____ and _____ and _____, _____ and _____, _____ and _____, _____ and _____.

The activity can be made into a game: any child who touches the wrong part of the body, or who sings during what should be a silent beat, is eliminated.

The activity becomes more interesting if you increase the speed of the song towards the end, when there are more actions than words.

Music score

shoulders knees and toes, knees and toes and eyes and ears and

mouth and nose. Head and shoulders knees and

toes. Knees and toes.

2. The Hokey-Cokey

Song	Action
Song	*Action*
You put your <u>right</u> <u>arm</u> <u>in</u>,	*Put your right arm into the circle*
you put your <u>right</u> <u>arm</u> <u>out</u>.	*Lift your right arm out of the circle*
<u>In</u> <u>out</u>, <u>in</u> <u>out</u>,	*Put your arm in the circle on 'in' and out again on 'out'*
you <u>shake</u> it <u>all</u> <u>about</u>.	*Shake right arm*
You <u>do</u> the <u>Hokey</u>-<u>Cokey</u>	*Make an arch with your hands and move it to the left and right*
and you <u>turn</u> <u>a</u>-<u>round</u>.	*Turn around*
<u>That</u>'s what it's <u>all</u> <u>about</u>.	*Mark time with feet*
Chorus	
<u>Oh</u>, Hokey-Cokey-<u>Cokey</u>.	*Join hands and walk into the middle of the circle, then back again*
(Repeat twice)	
<u>Knees</u> bend, <u>arms</u> stretch,	*Bend knees, stretch arms*
<u>Ra</u>, <u>ra</u>, <u>ra</u>.	*Shake fists on each 'ra'*

The song continues in the same vein, with *left arm*, *right leg*, *left leg*, then *whole self* in succeeding verses.

Music score

You put your right arm in you put your right arm out. In out, in out, you

shake it all a-bout. You do the Ho-key Co-key and you turn a-round. That's what it's all a-

bout. Oh, Ho-key Co-key Co-key. Oh, Ho-key Co-key Co-key. Oh, Ho-key Co-key Co-key

Knees bend, arms stretch, Ra-ra-ra.

Teacher's diary

Which rhyme did you try? Were the learners able to keep in rhythm? Are there any other rhymes which you can devise actions for? Can you think of other actions which fit rhymes?

Note

1. The rhymes given here are traditional. Two other sources of action rhymes for young children are *Game Songs with Professor Dogg's Troupe: 44 Songs and Games with Activities*, chosen by Harriet Powell with drawings by David McKee, A and C Black, 1985 (cassette available separately) and *Brown Bread and Butter: 70 songs, rhymes and games for children*, collected by Alison McMorland, Ward Lock, 1982.

35 Rapping

Level	Upper intermediate to advanced
Students	Teenage to young adult
Groups	Groups
Purpose	To familiarise learners with the regular stress patterns associated with some common suffixes in English
Text type	Teacher's chosen rap

In this activity

Learners brainstorm words with common suffixes, listen and sing along with a rap, then devise their own rap.

Preparation

Raps are a particular kind of rhyming popular song which is said rather than sung, usually to a backing track of drum beats. These backing tracks are easily made using electronic musical equipment, or they can be bought on cassette. The Sample teaching material is the song 'Mediate' by INXS, from their album *Kick* (Mercury 1987). The procedure uses this material, but can be adapted to fit other raps.

Procedure

1. Divide your learners into groups and tell them to think of as many words ending in -ate as they can. Set a time limit for this task, two or three minutes should be sufficient.

2. Ask each group to give you some of the words they thought of, and write these on the board.

3. Play the song and ask learners to listen hard and write down any -ate words they hear.

4. Give learners time to work in their groups to pool answers, then find out how many words they heard.

5. Give out copies of the rap, or show it on the overhead projector, for learners to check how many rhymes they spotted, before playing the rap again, with students singing along if they wish.

6. Now divide the learners into groups again, and set each group the task of devising their own rap. They can be given the same suffix, or different ones. Suffixes which are quite prevalent, and have regular stress include -ic, -ity and -ation. Set a time limit for this task, about fifteen minutes should be enough.

7. Hear each group's rap, performed by them in front of the class. They can do it to a backing track if you have one available, otherwise clapping or finger clicking in time to their beat will do just as well.

Sample teaching material

MEDIATE • • HALLUCINATE DESSEGREGATE MEDIATE ALLEVIATE TRY NOT TO HATE • LOVE YOUR MATE DON'T SUFFOCATE ON YOUR OWN HATE DESIGNATE YOUR LOVE AS FATE A ONE WORLD STATE AS HUMAN FREIGHT THE NUMBER EIGHT A WHITE BLACK STATE A GENTLE TRAIT THE BROKEN CRATE A HEAVY WEIGHT OR JUST TOO LATE LIKE PRETTY KATE HAS SEX ORNATE NOW DEVASTATE APPRECIATE DEPRECIATE FABRICATE EMULATE THE TRUTH DILATE SPECIAL DATE THE ANIMAL WE ATE GUILT DEBATE THE EDGE SERRATE A BETTER RATE THE YOUTH IRATE DELIBERATE • FASCINATE DEVIATE REINSTATE LIBERATE TOO MODERATE RECREATE OR DETONATE ANNIHILATE ATOMIC FATE • MEDIATE CLEAR THE STATE ACTIVATE NOW RADIATE A PERFECT STATE FOOD ON PLATE GRAVITATE THE EARTH'S OWN WEIGHT DESIGNATE YOUR LOVE AS FATE AT NINETY EIGHT WE ALL ROTATE • HALLUCINATE DESSEGREGATE MEDIATE ALLEVIATE TRY NOT TO HATE • LOVE YOUR MATE DON'T SUFFOCATE ON YOUR OWN HATE DESIGNATE YOUR LOVE AS FATE A ONE WORLD STATE AS HUMAN FREIGHT THE NUMBER EIGHT A WHITE BLACK STATE A GENTLE TRAIT THE BROKEN CRATE • A HEAVY WEIGHT OR JUST TOO LATE LIKE PRETTY KATE HAS SEX ORNATE NOW DEVASTATE APPRECIATE DEPRECIATE FABRICATE EMULATE THE TRUTH DILATE SPECIAL DATE THE ANIMALS WE ATE GUILT DEBATE THE EDGE SERRATE A BETTER RATE THE YOUTH IRATE DELIBERATE FASCINATE DEVIATE REINSTATE • LIBERATE • LIBERATE • LIBERATE • LIBERATE •

Teacher's diary

Was there evidence that this activity helped learners' stress placement? Would you change anything in the procedure for next time?

36 The poet speaks

Level	Intermediate to advanced
Students	Teenage to adult
Groups	Whole class, groups or pairs
Purpose	To improve pronunciation, to raise awareness of rhyme and rhythm
Text type	Teacher's poem

In this activity

Students look for rhymes in a poem, devise their own rhymes, then recite a poem together.

Preparation

You will need to find a poem with strong rhythm and regular rhyming scheme. The Sample teaching material is John Cooper Clarke's 'Nothing'.[1]

Procedure

1. Put a few words from your chosen poem on the board and ask your learners if they can think of other words which rhyme with them. For example, in the poem from the Sample teaching material, *flat*, *care* and *wall* might provoke any of the following rhymes from volunteers: mat, cat, hat; hair, bear, where; call, hall, etc.

2. Show your learners enough of the poem to show its regular rhyme scheme, either using the overhead projector or giving out photocopies of the relevant part of the poem. For the Sample teaching material, the first section as far as *nowt* will suffice.

3. Divide the class into groups of four, and ask them to underline the pairs of words that rhyme, then say what the pattern of rhyme is. Set a time limit for this task, about three minutes perhaps.

4. Before you give general feedback that there are rhymes in every alternate line, making an 'abab' pattern, ask one member of each group to tell you their answers. Point out the rhymes that aren't really rhymes, but make the poem interesting because of them – *anything* with *anything* and *nothing* with *nada* in the Sample teaching material.

5. Now give out copies of the rest of the poem, from which you have blanked out some rhymes. In the Sample teaching material, you would give out copies with *nowhere*, *one*, *gone* and *wall* blanked out (and perhaps *ends* also for more advanced classes). Ask your learners, working together in the same groups as before, to decide which words should go in the gaps. Set a time limit for this task, five minutes perhaps.

6. Before telling the class the actual missing items, ask one member of each group to give you the rhymes they have decided on. For the Sample teaching material, you will need to explain that *myself* with *else* and *ends* with *them* are false rhymes, and that *on* doesn't rhyme with *one* in the standard accent, although it does in Liverpool, where the poet comes from.

7. Now prepare for reciting the poem: number the learners in their groups, a,b,a,b. The 'a' students will recite the 'a' lines of the poem, and the 'b' students will recite the 'b' lines. This can either be done around the group of four students, each one taking a line in order, or it can be done in pairs, each pair sitting facing each other.

8. Allow the groups/pairs to practise reciting the poem, simultaneously, for a few minutes.

9. Now tell the class that they are all going to say the poem together, each student speaking the lines they have practised in time to your beat. Set up the beat – for the Sample it is $\frac{4}{4}$ ♩ ♩ ♩ 𝄽 , given by two slaps of your hands on your knees, one clap, and a rest. Get the rhythm going and invite learners to join in for a while before beginning the poem. Say the poem.

Teacher's diary

Were the learners able to produce rhymes for the poem easily? Did they produce any answers which showed that they had insufficient knowledge of spelling rules, or that they had confused one vowel sound with another? How did the students react to the recitation? Would you do anything differently next time?

Sample teaching material

nothing

nothing isn't anything
it's tasteless and it's flat
nothing if it's anything
is even less than that
i've got that certain nothing
no one can do without
the spanish call it nada
i call it nowt
i'd take the train but don't care
to travel by myself
all the way from nowhere
to get to nowhere else
nothing ever goes on
nothing never ends
say nothing to no one
it's nothing to do with them
nothing going on and on
nothing wall to wall
it happens once and then it's gone
leaving bugger all

Note
1.   From John Cooper Clarke, *Ten Years in an Open Necked Shirt*, Arrow Books, 1983.

37 Limerick jigsaws

Level   Upper intermediate to advanced

Students   Adults and young adults

Groups   Whole class, individuals or groups, depending on activity

Purpose   To improve learners' knowledge of, and ability to, rhyme

Text type   Teacher's chosen limericks

In this activity

Students reconstruct and/or complete limericks.

Preparation

Find four or five limericks to use with the class. Limericks are ideal for practis-
ing rhyme, because they follow a regular pattern and have predictable openings
(There was a . . . who . . .) and are therefore easy for learners to work with.
The Sample teaching material gives four of these humorous rhymes.

Procedure

1. Show on the overhead projector, or give copies of, 'There was a young man
    from Bengal' from the Sample teaching material. Recite it to the class, and
    explain to them that poems with this pattern are called limericks. Then
    proceed in one of the following ways:

Variation 1

2. Give each learner *one* line only of *one* of the three limericks in the sample.
    Learners mill about the room trying to find four other learners whose lines
    make up their limerick. For this variation you need fifteen learners, who
    together will make up the three limericks.

Variation 2

2. Jumble up the fifteen lines of the three limericks in the sample, photocopy them, and give copies to learners working in groups. Each group tries to unscramble the lines, so as to form the three original limericks.

Variation 3

2. Give out copies of the three sample limericks, minus their last line. Divide the learners into groups and ask them to try to complete the poems.

Variation 4

2. Divide the learners into groups of three or four, and give each group *one* line only from *one* of the three sample limericks. Each group should have a different line. Tell each group which line of the poem they have (e.g. if you have given out the line, 'One morning at one', tell the group that this is Line 3 of a limerick). Their task is to write the rest of the limerick.

3. After an appropriate time, bring the class together as a whole to pool their ideas, before distributing copies of the original limericks for comparison.

Sample teaching material

There was a young man from Bengal
Who went to a fancy dress ball.
He thought he would risk it
And go as a biscuit,
But a dog ate him up in the hall.

There was a young soldier called Ted,
Who spent too much time in his bed.
One morning at one
They fired the gun,
And later poor Ted was found dead.

There was an old man of Hong Kong
Who never did anything wrong.
He lay on his back,
With his head in a sack,
So his life was incredibly long.

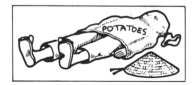

There was a young man of New York
Who ate his ice-cream with a fork.
People said, 'Oh my word!
He is really absurd.'
And they hit him with bits of white chalk.

Teacher's diary

Which variation did you try? How easily did the learners find rhymes? Why not run a limerick competition in your school?

38 Compound word stress

Level	Intermediate
Students	All ages
Groups	Whole class or groups
Purpose	To sensitise learners to the effect of accurate stress placement on communication
Text type	Teacher's list of compound nouns

In this activity

Learners practise varying stress so as to alter meaning.

Preparation

Make your own list of suitable compound nouns, or use the Sample teaching material for this activity.

Procedure

1. Distribute copies of your list of compound nouns. Model the first compound: firstly with stress on the first word, and then with stress on the second. Ask your learners to describe the effect on meaning of the change in stress placement, and to think up sentences to illustrate their answer.

2. Ask your learners to work in groups to discuss the rest of the compound nouns in the same way. For lower levels, the whole word list can be dealt with as a whole class activity, if preferred.

3. Bring the class together to hear the results of their discussions, and then, if the Sample teaching material was used, give the key.

Sample teaching material

Compound noun list

1. quiet room   2. black bird   3. green house   4. rain fall
5. light blue   6. foot rest

Key

Stress on first word	*Stress on second word*
The quiet room is for private study.	This is a nice, quiet room where we can talk.
There's a blackbird on the lawn.	Look at that big, black bird over there.
I grow tomatoes in the greenhouse.	My place is that little green house on the corner.
The rainfall is expected to increase.	Did the rain fall heavily?
He wore a light blue shirt with dark blue trousers.	He wore a light, blue shirt over cotton trousers.
Use the footrest if it's more comfortable.	Let that foot rest a while because you've sprained it badly.

Teacher's diary

How did the learners react to this activity? Were they able to imitate the shifting stress accurately? Would you change anything in the procedure for next time?

39 Guess the stress[1]

Level	Elementary to advanced
Students	All ages
Groups	Whole class
Purpose	To improve discrimination and production of word stress
Text type	Teacher's words and phrases

In this activity

Students engage in a communicative matching activity with other class members.

Preparation

You will need to prepare a card for each learner according to the variation you choose to try. Sample cards are given in the Sample teaching material for this activity.

Procedure[2]

1. Explain to the class that you are going to give everyone a piece of card with a word written on one side and a stress pattern on the other side. (The stress pattern can be indicated by drawing large and small circles or squares, as in the Sample teaching material.) Tell them that their word does *not* necessarily match the stress pattern on the other side of their card.

2. Tell the class that their task is to walk around the room and talk to other students in order to find a) a learner whose word matches their stress pattern and b) a learner whose stress pattern matches their word; for example, if the card has *computer* on one side and ■ ■ ■ ■ on the other side, it could be matched with ■ ■ ■ and *decoration*, respectively.

3. When most learners have found a match for each side of their card – fast finishers can be given another card – bring the class together for feedback: write on the board the stress patterns you used, and ask learners to form into groups according to the stress pattern of their word. Check that the learners have made the correct choices.

Variation 1

The procedure is as above, but the cards are only one sided – they are marked with *either* a word *or* a phrase. Students must match a word to a phrase with the identical stress pattern.

Variation 2

The procedure is as above, but again the cards are only one sided, marked with either a word or a phrase. Learners go around the class *walking* the stress of their word or phrase – a long stride for strong stress and a short stride for weak stress – until they find another learner whose stress pattern is identical to theirs.

Variation 3

The procedure is as above, but learners *clap* the rhythm of their word or phrase, for other learners to guess whether it matches their own.

Sample teaching material

Stress pattern	Word list
▪ ▪ ▪ ■ ▪	congratulations, felicitations, environmental
▪ ■ ▪	together, electric, terrific, September
▪ ▪ ■	refugee, employee, Japanese, engineer
▪ ▪ ■ ▪	satisfaction, monumental, manufacture
■ ▪ ▪	beautiful, crazily, northerner, colourless, horrible, autocrat

Sample material for Variations 1, 2 and 3 is as above, plus the following phrases:

Stress pattern	Phrase list
▪ ▪ ▪ ◼ ▪	she's at the station it's in the paper they're on the telly I hadn't noticed
▪ ◼ ▪	it's over your mother you're joking
▪ ▪ ◼	it's a lie quite a lot in the sky
▪ ▪ ◼ ▪	he's amazing can't believe it two pounds twenty come on Sunday
◼ ▪ ▪	there it is ask him, then give her one

Teacher's diary

Which variation did you try? How quickly were the learners able to match the patterns? Did they volunteer any words or phrases of their own to match?

Notes
1. Appendix 6 gives rules for stress placement which have been used in this activity.
2. Adapted from ideas by Tessa Woodward and Eva Jonai, given at seminars organised by IATEFL and SEAL, respectively.

40   Stress pictures

Level	Intermediate and above
Students	All ages
Groups	Groups
Purpose	To improve knowledge of stress placement in English words
Text type	Teacher's word list

In this activity

Learners undertake a problem-solving activity matching stress patterns to colour and/or shape.

Preparation

Prepare a list of about twenty words of three or four syllables, which have different stress patterns, or use the Sample teaching material. Bring to class a set of cuisenaire rods, or alternatively some gummed paper shapes, which you will use to represent three degrees of 'stress'. (See Sample teaching material.)

Procedure[1]

1. Tell your class that you are going to divide them into groups. Each group will be given some rods (or gummed paper shapes) and a word list. Their task will be to classify the items on the word list according to the appropriate stress pattern.

2. Demonstrate some different stress patterns to the class; for example: Using cuisenaire rods, you could represent *computer*, *marvellous*, *refugee* by black rods for strong stress, red rods for medium stress, and white rods for weak stress:

□	▐	□	▐	□	▓	▓	□	▐
white	black	white,	black	white	red,	red	white	black
com	pu	ter	mar	vel	lous	re	fu	gee

Using gummed paper shapes, you could represent the three degrees of stress by circles, squares and triangles; or large, medium and small squares; or various colours.

3. Give out copies of your chosen word list to each group and some rods or paper shapes. Ask everyone to look at the first item on the list and decide what stress pattern it has. How can they represent this with their rods, or shapes?

4. Now set the groups to work on the rest of the word list. Give help to individuals as needed during the activity: they should end up with a set of four stress patterns, and a list of which items correspond with which.

5. After the learners have completed the task, bring them together to check that they have the correct answers. Have they been able to deduce any rules for stress placement?

6. Follow up: If you used the Sample teaching material, invite your learners to chant the words with similar endings, so as to emphasise the stress placement (e.g. *barbaric, adoption, astonish*, etc.). If they have devised rules of their own, how do *entrepreneur* and *Vietnamese* fit?

Sample teaching material

The four stress patterns are:

a) weak weak strong
b) weak strong weak
c) strong weak medium
d) medium weak strong weak

The words to be classified, in random order, are:

1. mountaineer, 2. barbaric, 3. realise, 4. satisfaction, 5. constitution, 6. fortitude, 7. electric, 8. picturesque, 9. adoption, 10. gratitude, 11. monumental, 12. connoisseur, 13. raconteur, 14. liquefy, 15. astonish, 16. revelation, 17. governmental, 18. detonate, 19. acoustic, 20. employee, 21. detainee, 22. objection, 23. graduate, 24. contraception, 25. acolyte, 26. manufacture, 27. occasion, 28. engineer, 29. arabesque, 30. velarise, 31. admonish, 32. sybaritic, 33. indecisive, 34. terrific, 35. coalesce, 36. Japanese, 37. protective.

Key:
Pattern a) 1., 8., 10., 12., 13., 14., 20., 21., 28., 29., 35., 36.
Pattern b) 2., 7., 9., 15., 19., 22., 27., 31., 34., 37.
Pattern c) 3., 6., 18., 23., 25., 30.
Pattern d) 4., 5., 11., 16., 17., 24., 26., 32., 33.

Teacher's diary

Were the students able to classify the words correctly? What rules did they devise?

Note
1.   The stress rules illustrated here are to be found in Appendix 6.

41 Shifting stress dominoes

Level	Upper intermediate to advanced
Students	Adults
Groups	Groups
Purpose	To demonstrate the relationship of certain prefixes and suffixes to stress patterning in English
Text type	Teacher's word list

In this activity

Learners play a card game to discover rules for stress shift.

Preparation

Using the Sample teaching material, or similar material of your own choosing, make three sets of cards for each group of learners: one set of word cards and two sets of suffix cards, as shown in the Sample teaching material. A different colour for each of the three sets would be ideal.

Procedure

1. Demonstrate the game in front of the class to begin with:

    a) Explain that the game is to be played in groups of three. Each of the three learners has one of the coloured sets of cards, which he/she shuffles and places face downwards.

    b) The person with the word cards begins, and turns over the top card of the set (e.g. *photograph*).

    c) The next player – it does not matter which, since both of the other card sets are identical – turns over the top card of the set (e.g. -er). If this suffix fits the word turned over by the previous player, these two cards are left face up – in this case *photographer* is possible.

    d) The third player then turns up the top card from the third set. If this suffix also fits, then all three cards are placed to one side, in order. In our example case, there is no suffix that can fit after 'photographer', so only the two cards, 'photograph' and '-er' can be placed to one side here. However, some three-card combinations are possible (e.g. 'danger' + 'ous' + 'ly').

e) Each time a combination is made, learners say how it would be pronounced, and where the stress should fall (e.g. <u>pho</u>tograph but photo<u>gra</u>pher).

f) If the second player's suffix cannot fit, the turn passes to the third player, whose suffix may fit instead. The game ends when no more combinations are possible.

2. Set the groups to work, playing the game simultaneously, whilst you monitor their work as needed. A dictionary may be useful too.

3. If appropriate refer the learners to the stress rules in Appendix 6.

Sample teaching material

Each group needs to work with this three-set pack:

Set 1: Word cards (Colour 1)		Set 2: Suffix cards (Colour 2)	Set 3: Suffix cards (Colour 3)
photograph	hap(py)(i)	-ly	-ly
seismograph	synonym	-y	-y
microscop(e)	danger	-er	-er
biograph	analog(ue)	-ness	-ness
hexagon	light	-ful	-ful
origin	parent	-less	-less
brother	hope	-al	-al
thought	continent	-ous	-ous

Teacher's diary

Were the learners able to pronounce the stress correctly? Were they able to make hypotheses of their own about possible rules for stress placement? Would you change anything in the procedure for next time?

SECTION IV

WORKING WITH ENGLISH INTONATION

Introduction

Intonation has been compared to the planet Mars, 'just out of reach and shrouded in mystery.'[1] Part of our problem with it is our perception: intonation is a fleeting phenomenon which is hard to catch or to bring into conscious awareness. There is also no one-to-one correspondence between what is said and how it is realised in intonation: an utterance of four or five words may be said with as many different intonation patterns as there are words. Intonation poses problems for teachers because there are no 'rules', only 'tendencies', but we can take heart from the fact that there seem to be 'intonation universals', which involve falls for 'certainty' and rises for 'uncertainty' or 'questioning' in most languages of the world.[2]

There are, however, many language-specific aspects of intonation that a learner would benefit from studying. There has been a renewal of interest in teaching intonation, along with recent and current trends in linguistic theory. The use of authentic conversational text as material for language learning has meant a new focus on stress and intonation, as has the functional approach to language teaching and we are now legitimately concerned as much with *how* to say something as with *what* to say. It is true that attitude and purpose are conveyed in English by subtle variations in stress and intonation. Foreigners vary in their perception of English stress and intonation and some of our European neighbours may find our vocal range much wider than theirs and our stresses stronger, whilst Far Eastern learners may find English speech monotonous, with far fewer peaks and valleys than their own, and African learners may notice that our stresses are fewer and less strong than theirs.

Sadly, no language has a writing system which adequately represents the rhythms and melodies of its utterances, though in English punctuation marks, italics, underscoring and upper case letters can go some way towards achieving this. It is therefore important that learners see the role of intonation as the 'punctuation of spoken English' (see Activity 44). One point to remember is that in an English utterance the largest degree of pitch movement coincides with the main stress, and *both* occur in the *last stressed syllable* of the utterance, for example:

What did you have for DINner?

I had BEEF.

Was it GOOD?

Linguists have divided intonation into various parameters. Firstly, there is the way in which an English utterance is broken up into chunks, for example: 'I'm going to London on Saturday' can be said quickly all in one breath – one chunk – or the 'on Saturday' part can be said as an afterthought – two chunks. These 'chunks' are called 'tone units' and chunking in general is called 'tonality'. (Activities 51 and 52 deal with this aspect of intonation.)

Then there is the question of where to put the emphasis, for example: 'I'm going to LONdon on Saturday' (not Manchester) or 'I'm going to London on SATurday' (not Friday). This aspect has been referred to as ' tonicity' and the emphasis itself may be called 'stress' or 'prominence'. (Activity 43 deals with this.)

Thirdly, there is the way in which the voice rises or falls, the tune, which is usually referred to as 'tone'. Two broad categories – 'falling' and 'rising' – are recognised, with subdivisions into 'fall-rise' and 'rise-fall'. As well as the 'certainty'/'uncertainty' distinction already referred to, a falling tone is usually used for *new* information and a rising tone for something already mentioned, and thus *shared* information. (Activities 50 and 54 practise these distinctions.) Finally, 'key' is a term used to refer to the relative pitch levels of parts of utterances.[3] Compare the effect of saying 'I'm going to LONdon' with a low falling pitch, with saying 'I'm going to LONdon' with a high falling pitch – the high version sounds surprised, as though going to London is a rare occurrence, whereas the low version sounds as though going to London is the most natural thing in the world. (Key differences are practised in Activities 46 and 48.) (Appendix 7 gives some 'rules of thumb' which may be useful when teaching intonation.)

Notes
1. B. Jenner and B. Bradford, 'Intonation through listening' in *Modern English Teacher*, 10, pp. 38–42.
2. See A. Cruttenden, 'Falls and Rises, Meanings and Universals' in *Journal of linguistics*, 17 (1981); and Arnolt, Horst *et al.*, 'A neurological view of prosody and its importance in human communication' in *Die Neueren Sprachen* (Frankfurt am Main) 85, 5/6 (1986), pp. 581–610.
3. D. Brazil, in *The Communicative Value of Intonation*, ELR (University of Birmingham) 1985.

42 I got rhythm

Level	Elementary to advanced, depending on input
Students	All ages
Groups	Individuals, pairs or whole class
Purpose	To train learners to listen for cues related to stress patterns in English, in order to help understanding of English spoken at some speed
Text type	Teacher's text

In this activity

Learners use dictation as a vehicle for training their ears to 'sound shapes'.

Introduction

It can be helpful for learners to have some way of recording the 'sound shape' of a word they have heard but not understood. The system I use for this is a dot for a weak stress and a dash for a strong stress, i.e. the words 'carefully' and 'disappointing' would be represented respectively as: ▬ ● ● and ● ● ▬ ●. It is easy to use this method of notation at speed, during a lecture or talk, and in this way learners have a 'sound clue' to the word they missed, so that they have a better chance of working out what must have been said. This activity describes one way of training learners to be aware of word stress.

Preparation

Prepare a text for dictation, by substituting some multisyllabic words with their 'sound shapes', e.g. instead of 'A new phone book will be delivered this week to telephone subscribers', you could read, 'A new phone book will be DIDADEE this week to DADIDEE subscribers', and so on. Prepare a version of the dictation for each student: this will give all the text *except* for the multisyllabic words you have chosen to substitute, and these will be represented by gaps for the students to fill.

Procedure[1]

1. Distribute copies of your gapped text.

2. Dictate the text, asking students to listen and mark the sound shapes they hear, using the system of dots and dashes as explained in the introduction to this activity.

3. After you have dictated the text, a second and/or third time as required, ask students to work in pairs or groups to check the sound shapes they have recorded.

4. Ask the students, working in pairs or groups again, to write into their texts possible words to fit the sound shapes of the substituted words, e.g. in the sample sentence, 'DADIDEE subscribers' could be 'various subscribers' or 'targeted subscribers' just as well as 'telephone subscribers', the original version.

5. With the class as a whole, ask for feedback from the words discussed, explaining if necessary where stress has been wrongly placed, before giving the 'correct' version for comparison.

Teacher's diary

Were learners able to use the shorthand system proposed? How accurate were they? Did any of the words they volunteered surprise you?

Note
1. This technique is especially good for alerting learners to shifting stress in context. Compare 'disapPOInting', 'everLASting', 'underNEATH' to 'a DISappointing reSULT', 'to his Everlasting CREdit', 'he was UNderneath the BEDclothes'.

43   Playing with stress shift

Level	Beginner to advanced
Students	All ages
Groups	Groups, pairs or whole class
Purpose	To help learners attend to shifting stress placement
Text type	Simple one-word prompts, or short phrases

In this activity

Students perform a chain of responses to practise stress shift.

Introduction

As a general rule, new information is stressed and old or shared information is unstressed in English. This means that a word appearing in conversation for the first time (new) will have stress, whereas a word which has already been mentioned will have no stress when it is repeated (old). This activity practises this feature.

Preparation

Decide whether you want to work with one-word or two-word prompts, compounds or short phrases, and prepare a few examples, as in the Sample teaching material for this activity.

Procedure

1. Arrange the class into evenly numbered groups. The ideal number for a group is eight members. The members of each group form two rows, facing each other, a 'Number 1' row, sitting opposite a 'Number 2' row, as shown overleaf.

1	1	1	1	1
2	2	2	2	2

If the furniture in your classroom is fixed, you can ask some of the rows to turn round and face the row behind.

2. Demonstrate the game with one group: call out 'twenty-one' and point to the first learner from Number 1 row, who must change the *first* element only, and stress it (e.g. THIRty-one). Then point to the first learner from Number 2 row, who must then change the *second* element only, and stress it (e.g. thirty-TWO). The turn then passes to the next learner from Number 1 row, who again changes the *first* element (e.g. FORty-two) and from there to the next learner from Number 2 row, who must change only the second element again (e.g. forty-SEven). Turns continue in sequence for as long as learners can keep going. Learners need not choose to increase the amount each time, they can decrease it too. A typical chain might be: twenty-one – THIRty-one – thirty-TWO – FORty-two – forty-SEven – THIRty-seven – thirty-FOUR – FIFty-four – fifty-NINE – TWENty-nine, etc.

3. Set the groups to work simultaneously. One learner in each group begins by saying 'twenty-one' and the game continues as described above. Monitor the groups whilst they play.

4. Follow up: When the class has become proficient at manipulating stress shift on simple numerals, try the same technique for two-word utterances, then whole phrases; for example:

Two-word food chain: chicken soup – toMAto soup – tomato SAlad – BEEF salad – beef ROLL – CHEESE roll – cheese SANDwich – toMAto sandwich, etc.

Whole phrase relations and professions chain: My aunt's a hairdresser – My UNcle's a hairdresser – My uncle's a meCHAnic – My BROther's a mechanic – My brother's a TEACher, etc.

Teacher's diary

Which variation did you try? Did the learners improve in their ability to apply stress shift? Can you think of other words or phrases to practise this feature?

44 Punctuation card game

Level	Elementary
Students	Young learners
Groups	Whole class, teams or pairs
Purpose	To help learners discriminate between falling and rising tones, and between different variations in pitch and loudness. To help learners produce these features appropriately themselves.
Text type	Learners' own words or phrases

In this activity

Learners play an elimination game to practise the relationship between intonation and punctuation.

Preparation

For each team, produce three punctuation cards, as in the Sample teaching material for this activity. These should be of at least A5 size.

Procedure

1. Divide your learners into several teams, and give out a set of punctuation cards to each team. Tell the learners that you are going to say someone's name in three ways, and they must copy you. First, say the name as if you were simply answering the question: What's your name?:

    Mary.

    Next, say it as if it's a question:

    Mary?

Finally, say it as if it's a command, very loud, starting high and ending low:

Mary!

Hold up the corresponding punctuation card as you say each one.

2. Now say the name several times and ask teams to hold up the appropriate punctuation card for each. Check whether the team responses are correct and repeat if not.

3. Now call out a succession of names – those of class members are ideal for motivation. After each name, teams show the card which they think corresponds to the way you said the name. Eliminate any team which guesses wrongly, and continue until one team only remains. As the learners become accustomed to the game you could begin to call names sometimes as both command *and* question:

Mary!?

Both exclamation and question marks would need to be raised in response to this fourth type of intonation.

4. Finally, set the teams to work simultaneously on their own, with one member of each team taking the role of teacher and the rest guessing the punctuation.

Variations

1. Step 4 can be done as pair work, with one member of the pair taking the role of teacher, the other that of guesser, then changing roles.

2. Short prepositional phrases can be used instead of single words once the principles of the game are understood (e.g. on the table, under the chair).

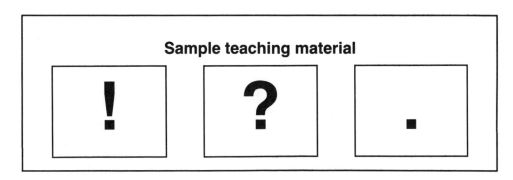

Sample teaching material

Teacher's diary

How did the learners respond to this activity? Were there signs that learners were improving in their ability to hear tones? Can you think of further exercises which could build on this activity?

45 Calling choices

Level	Elementary to intermediate
Students	All ages
Groups	Pairs
Purpose	To improve learners' intonation of lists
Text type	Open dialogues

In this activity

Learners respond to each others' questions using appropriate intonation.

Preparation

Use the Sample teaching material for this activity. You will need one copy per pair of students.

Procedure

1. Ask your learners some introductory questions from the Sample teaching material; for example, What television programmes do you like?, What do you like doing in the evenings?

2. Go over the answers again, pointing out the intonation; for example,

   Fernando, you said, 'I like reading, watching TV and playing football.'[1]

3. Divide the class into pairs. Give out the incomplete dialogues and demonstrate the first few with one or two students; for example,

   What sort of fruit have you got? – Oranges, apples, pears and bananas, etc.

4. Now set the pairs to work simultaneously to try out the rest of the material. They should swap roles, so that both students in the pair have a chance to use the intonation pattern.

5. After the exercise, invite your learners to empty their pockets or bags and to use the 'intonation of lists' to describe the contents; for example,

I've got a pen, a tissue, a note book and some money.

6. Follow up: There is another type of 'intonation of lists' which is used when there is an unlimited number of choices. This is a string of rising tones, with no fall at the end; for example,

I like reading, watching TV, playing football, . . .
You could ask your learners to try the dialogues again, using this second type of intonation pattern.

Sample teaching material

Students think of suitable responses in the form of lists.
1. What sort of fruit have you got?
   We've got ⤴ ⤴ ⤴ and ⤵
2. What's on the menu today?
3. I'd like a sweater. What sizes do you have?/What colours?
4. Which bus should I catch?
5. How much are the tickets for the theatre tonight?
6. What do you like doing in the evenings?
7. What television programmes do you like?
8. Do you play any sports?
9. Who have you invited to the party?

Teacher's diary

Were the students able to use the intonation of lists correctly? Did you try the follow-up activity? Can you think of other prompts which might give rise to the same intonation pattern?

Note
1. The 'intonation of lists' is normally a rise for each item on the list except the last, where

there is a fall: I'd like a coffee, a tea and a chocolate.

46   Testing assumptions

Level   Intermediate

Students   Teenage to adult

Groups   Whole class or groups

Purpose   To help learners use falling tunes effectively and with appropriate vocal range

Text type   Learners' own questions

In this activity

Learners play a question and answer game in which both questions and answers have falling tones.

Preparation

None.

Procedure

1. Choose a volunteer from the class. Other students must think of one true fact about the volunteer and write it down. It may be appropriate to give prompts for the students such as likes/dislikes, school life, family, sports/ hobbies, future plans.

2. Ask a few individual students for the facts which they wrote down, and turn them into a tag question; for example, if the students wrote, 'She has two brothers' and 'She plays the guitar', then write on the board,

    You have two brothers, don't you?
    and

    You play the guitar, don't you?

Model these questions (with two falling tones, as marked, because the information is thought to be correct).

3. Ask learners to form questions from their 'facts', using the models on the board for reference, and to practise putting their questions to the volunteer (who does not answer at this point). Correct intonation as required.

4. Now work with the volunteer, putting some of the students' questions from Step 3. If the answer is as expected, the volunteer should reply with a low, flat, falling tone:

   ➤Yes, I ➤ do.

   If the answer is not as expected, the volunteer should reply indignantly, with a much wider vocal range:
   You have two brothers, don't you?

   No. I have one brother.

5. Now invite the learners themselves to put their questions to the volunteer, who must respond appropriately.

6. Now the game begins. Ask for a second volunteer to come and sit in front of the class. The other learners must think of five tag questions for this second volunteer, to which they think they already know the answer. Choose individuals to put their five questions. If the volunteer has to raise her voice and give an unexpected answer, the questioner gains no points at all, but if she gives an expected answer (i.e. with low falling tone) the questioner gains a point. The game continues with other volunteers and other questions.

Variation

The game can be played in small groups with one volunteer per group.

Teacher's diary

Were the learners able to ask and answer with appropriate intonation? Did you make a note of the inappropriate intonation contours, for further work?

---

47 Over and over again

Level	Intermediate to advanced
Students	Teenage to adult
Groups	Groups or pairs
Purpose	To show learners the value of paraphrasing when communicating in English and to give practice in varying intonation in order to vary meaning
Text type	Teacher's prompts

In this activity

Learners play a game in which they repeat identical information using a different form of words.

Introduction

In English, if you simply answer a question with 'yes' or 'no', this is not enough to sound interested and leave the way open to further conversation. It is better to reply by saying the same thing in a different way; for example,

A: Lovely day, isn't it?
B: Yes, beautiful/Yes, wonderful.

If your reply is said with low pitch, you are simply agreeing. If your reply is said with high pitch, then you are agreeing, but also saying that what you have agreed is a surprising fact.

Compare:

A: Lovely day, isn't it?

B: Yes, beautiful.

with:

A: Lovely day, isn't it?

B: Yes, beautiful.

Here is a group activity to practise varying vocal range.

Preparation

Write about six suitable questions – examples are given in the Sample teaching material for this activity. You will need one copy of the set of questions for each student.

Procedure

1. Give out the list of questions and allow students time to think of how they could respond to each by paraphrasing. As an example model the first one yourself: Lovely day, isn't it?; and invite your students to volunteer responses (e.g. Yes, fantastic; Yes, gorgeous). Say these responses yourself with a) low fall and b) high fall and invite your students to comment on the difference. Allow students to rehearse these responses in different ways.

2. Divide the class into groups of three – two of the students will carry out the task, and one will observe and comment.

3. Explain the procedure: one student reads the first question; a second student responds with a paraphrase; the third student, observing, says whether or not he/she thinks the response sounded surprised, and checks with the second student to see if the desired effect had been achieved.

4. Set the class to work: the original pair of students complete all the two-line dialogues, with comments by the third students.

5. Students change roles, so that, at the end of the activity, each student has had a chance a) to initiate, b) to respond, and c) to comment.

6. Invite individuals to try out their dialogues for the class to guess whether the response is one of surprise or of simple agreement. Correct intonation as needed.

Sample teaching material

1. Lovely day, isn't it?

2. Horrid weather, isn't it?

3. That woman's so elegant, don't you think?

4. Have you given up cigarettes?

5. Did you know she's expecting twins?

6. I do hate this game, don't you?

Teacher's diary

Was there any evidence that the students were improving their vocal range? Did the students develop an ability to monitor their intonation more accurately?

48 Highlighting[1] picture differences

Level	Elementary to advanced
Students	All ages
Groups	Pairs
Purpose	To help learners understand and produce the particular pattern of stress and intonation which occurs when talking about differences
Text type	Teacher's picture cards

In this activity

Students work in pairs to discover differences between two pictures.

Introduction

In spoken English, when we give new information we use a falling tone. When responding to new information with more new information, we use a high falling tone, combined with increased emphasis and loudness. Here is an activity to practise falling tones and high falling tones. It also practises shifting stress.

Preparation

Find some pictures from magazines or catalogues, or use photographs, and sort them into pairs which are quite similar in content. You will need at least one picture for each student (you could photocopy some to make up the numbers). Photocopy the Sample teaching material for this activity, which shows two photos with several similarities, but also a few differences. You will also need copies of the transcript of two native speakers performing the activity, given in the sample material.

Procedure

1. Divide the class into two halves. Give one half of the class a copy of Picture A, and the other half a copy of Picture B. Read aloud the sample transcript or, better still, pre-record the dialogue, and play a tape recording of this activity. Tell learners to listen for where the speakers' voices rise higher and get louder on individual words.

2. After the reading, or tape recording, show the class the first few phrases from the transcript as examples. Invite learners to repeat, mimicking the stress and intonation patterns; for example,

    A: There's a GIRL in my picture. (low fall = new information)

    B: There's a girl in MY picture TOO, etc. (high fall = more new – and slightly surprising – information)

3. Now pair the learners according to their pictures. Each learner with Picture A sits with a learner with Picture B. They talk about their pictures, as in the dialogue. They will not be able to remember much of the dialogue at this stage, but they are free to imitate as much as they can remember and/or make up their own dialogue about the differences.

4. Give out the transcript, marked for intonation, and read or play the dialogue again so that learners can listen with the transcript. Then give a minute or so for pairs to read the transcript aloud to each other.

5. Now give out your own chosen picture pairs – one to each pair of learners – and ask them to perform the same task as before with these new pictures. Monitor the learners' intonation as they do this. As pairs of learners finish with one set of pictures, swap them for another set, using any spare sets if learners complete the task at different rates.

6. Finally, invite some pairs of learners to come to the front of the class and perform their dialogues. Record these dialogues so you can then play back to see whether the intonation patterns are appropriate.

Variation

With young learners, you may omit Step 4 above.

Sample teaching material

A: There's a GIRL in my picture.

B: There's a girl in MY picture TOO.

A: Mine's SITting on a DONkey.

B: Mine's sitting on a TRIcycle.

A: Mine's SMIling.

B. Mine's smiling TOO.

A: Mine's wearing a DRESS.

B: Mine's wearing a JUMPer and a SKIRT.

A: Mine's wearing a WATCH.

B: Mine ISn't wearing a watch.

A: Mine's wearing WHITE SOCKS.

B: My girl isn't wearing ANy socks.

A: Mine's got a RIBbon in her hair.

B: Mine's got a HAIRclip in HERS.

Note: This transcript can also be used to show that old information is unstressed: 'girl', 'sitting', 'smiling', 'watch', 'socks' are stressed on first appearance but not on second.

Teacher's diary

Were the learners able to use stress and intonation appropriately?
Were they able to use them in their *own* dialogues as well as when
reading from the scripted dialogue?

Note
1.   Highlighting is a term used by Barbara Bradford in *Intonation in Context*. (See Further
      reading in the Introduction to this book.)

49　Counting out an argument

Level	Advanced
Students	Teenage to adult
Groups	Pairs or groups
Purpose	To show the relationship between what is said and how it is said. To teach the effect of widening and narrowing vocal range.
Text type	Students' own dialogues

In this activity

Students act out wordless dialogues, then script them and act them again.

Introduction

This is a technique used in psychodrama[1] to enable people to cope with conflict. Here, the technique of wordless dialogue is used so that learners can concentrate on intonation, but the conflict scenario is chosen so that learners can be personally and emotionally involved with what they are enacting, and thus be more likely to use the intonational features needed.

Preparation

Choose an extract on audio or videotape in which an argument happens. A lighthearted one is best. You will need a transcript of this for each learner.

Procedure

1. Warm-up phase: Tell your learners that they are going to work through a scenario with you and with one another. The scenario is a simple shopping situation in which someone goes into a shop to buy something, chooses what she wants, buys it and leaves. The learners will work in pairs: one will

be the shop assistant, the other the shopper. However, the realisation of this scenario is to be spoken in numbers, not words. Demonstrate the activity with one learner; for example:

Number dialogue	Rough translation
Assistant: Three four seven?	Can I help you?
Shopper: Two seven twenty.	I'd like a shirt, please.
Assistant: Fifty. Eight nine ten?	Certainly. Plain or patterned?
Shopper: Eleven. Two. Twelve thirteen?	Plain. This is nice. How much is it?
Assistant: Fifteen three.	£20.
Shopper: Seventy. Nine.	I'll take it. Thanks.
Assistant: Ten. Twenty!	Thank you. Bye!

Now set pairs of learners to work simultaneously on this scenario. They can swap roles if time allows. At the end of the activity, ask learners what they bought.

2. Exercise proper, argument phase: Tell your learners that now they have experienced the technique of counting a dialogue, they are going to work on another scenario: one learner meets the other, at home or elsewhere. The two have not met for a long time. They engage in pleasant conversation at first, but then an argument develops and becomes quite heated. Finally though, the conflict is resolved and the two are the best of friends again.

3. Allow the learners time, individually, to think of a situation in their lives which might fit the argument scenario. It is important that everyone should do this alone and silently, without letting anyone else know what they are thinking.

4. Now pair learners together to act out their scenario using only numbers, as before. Each learner does this without knowing the detail of their partner's scenario, but the overall pattern of calm leading to conflict, leading to calm again is common. Tell learners that they may feel they want to use numbers in hundreds and thousands when they reach the height of the argument. Set the pairs to work, simultaneously.

5. After an appropriate time spent on the task, ask one or two pairs to act out their number drama. Tape record them if possible. Play back the tape and invite learners to say what happens to the voice intonation during the argument phase and then during the calm phase. (Some elements are: heavier stresses, raised pitch, increased volume, greater vocal range for the argument – reversed for the return to calm.)

6. Now let the learners discuss with their partner exactly what they were acting. They may find that they were portraying completely different situations. When I tried this activity recently, one woman said a girlfriend of hers had come to the house for a meal and complained about the cooking. Her partner had met someone who had accused her of speaking rudely about her husband!

7. Set the pairs to work again, this time to put words to the scenario they have just enacted in numbers. They must choose *one* of the two individual scenarios to work on. They should pay particular attention to the features of intonation discussed in Step 5: they should a) decide exactly where the argument is to be most heated and thus display greatest vocal range and loudness, and b) make their voices very calm and quiet at the end, with narrow vocal range.

8. After an appropriate time, ask one or two pairs to perform their drama for the others.

9. Now play your chosen taped argument and ask learners to listen to the intonation used. Give out transcripts of the taped extract, and invite learners, working in pairs, to practise reading the transcript aloud. Then play the tape again, so that learners can listen with the transcript.

Teacher's diary

Were the learners able to improve their ability to make changes in their vocal range? Can you think of other scenarios which you might use for the same purpose?

Note
1. Some interesting ways of using psychodrama to resolve family tensions are discussed by Ivan Sokolov and Deborah Hutton in *The Parents Book*, Thorson Publishers Ltd, 1988.

50 Afterthoughts

Level   Intermediate to advanced

Students   Teenage to adult

Groups   Pairs

Purpose   To train learners in the communicative use of the low rising tone.[1]

Text type   Student-generated questions and teacher's 'afterthoughts'

In this activity

Learners play a group question and answer game to practise using falling and low rising tones effectively.

Introduction

When we answer a question, we are giving new information. In standard English, new information is given in a falling tone, but too many falling tones in our intonation make us appear over-direct and over-assertive. When answering a series of questions, we may therefore try to moderate the effect of the straight falling tone by adding a tag to our straight answer. Compare the effect of the two sets of responses below:

Question	Response
What's your name?	Linda Taylor.
And where do you live?	In Nottingham.
Have you lived there long?	Nearly a year.

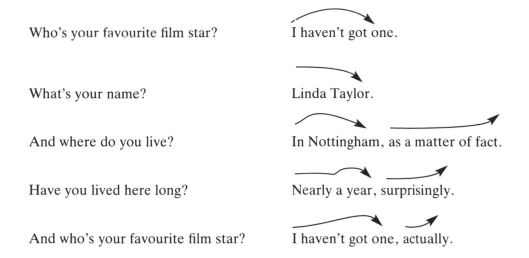

Who's your favourite film star?   I haven't got one.

What's your name?   Linda Taylor.

And where do you live?   In Nottingham, as a matter of fact.

Have you lived here long?   Nearly a year, surprisingly.

And who's your favourite film star?   I haven't got one, actually.

The following is a paired activity to practise the softening effect of adding tagged low rising tones to statements.

Preparation

Prepare your own list of 'afterthoughts' or use the ones in the Sample teaching material for this activity.

Procedure

1. Tell your learners that they are going to ask and answer questions about themselves. Divide the class into two, four or six groups, and ask them to work together to devise a set of ten general questions which they would like to ask other members of the class. Set a time limit for this, and give the groups some questions from the Sample teaching material for this activity if they need help getting started.

2. With the whole class, invite learners to ask *you* questions from their lists. Answer with straight falling tone and no tag, as in the first set of responses in the Introduction to this activity. Then invite learners to repeat the same questions. This time, answer each one with a tag from the list of sample afterthoughts, in the manner of the second set of responses in the Introduction to this activity. Invite learners to say whether they think you sounded more friendly the second time. (You should have!)

3. Now arrange the groups so that half of them are 'interviewers' and the other half are 'interviewees'. Give the list of afterthoughts (see Sample

teaching material) to the interviewees. In open class, invite an interviewer to put a question to one of the interviewees. The question should be answered, with low rising intonation, using a tag from the afterthoughts list. Repeat the process with two or three more interviewers and interviewees.

4. Reform the groups into pairs, so that one interviewer sits with one interviewee. They conduct an interview, then swap roles, so that each learner has practised the low rising intonation needed in answering questions. Monitor the pairs whilst this activity is in progress.

5. As consolidation, invite several pairs to act out their interviews. Correct intonation if needed.

Sample teaching material

'Interviewer' role: Sample questions

Where do you live? What's your favourite food? What kind of music do you like? How often do you go to the cinema? What do you do in the evenings? Have you got any children/brothers/sisters? What do you think of American films? Do you like spaghetti? What do you hate most about the English?

'Interviewee' role: Sample 'afterthoughts'

in fact, actually, really, if you know what I mean, in a manner of speaking, if you really want to know, I'm afraid, as a matter of fact, to be honest with you, if I'm honest, surprisingly, normally, usually, to tell you the truth, if you can believe it, I think.

Teacher's diary

Were the learners able to use the low rising intonation successfully? Did they sound less direct when doing so?

Note
1. For learners who sound abrupt and aggressive, accurate use of this tone will soften the effect they have on their hearers, and enable them to get what they want instead of a cold shoulder.

51   Monologue restyle

Level	Upper intermediate to advanced
Students	Young adult, adult
Groups	Groups
Purpose	To help learners appreciate the effects of varying declamatory styles, and to use the styles themselves with appropriate intonation
Text type	Teacher's chosen news report, play extract and fairy story

In this activity

Learners experiment with matching appropriate and inappropriate intonation to different genres of monologue, and play a related guessing game.

Preparation

Gather some news reports, play extracts, and fairy stories of your own, or use the ones given as Sample teaching material for this activity. You will need copies for each student. Tape recordings of the examples would be useful.

Procedure

1. Play short extracts from your chosen tape-recorded news report, fairy story and play excerpt. Invite your learners to tell you about the differences in the way they are spoken. (If no recordings are available, read the Sample extracts yourself.)

2. Divide the class into several groups of four. Give out copies of the Sample teaching material, or your own similar extracts, and invite learners, in pairs, to read them to one another with appropriate intonation.

3. Call on several learners to read one of the extracts. Correct intonation as needed.

4. Now read one of your extracts to the learners, but this time using an inappropriate intonation style (e.g. read the play extract as a news report, or the news report as a fairy story). Invite your learners to say a) whether what you read was a news report, a fairy story or a play, and b) which intonation style you used.

5. Set the groups to work on the following task: Each member of the group must choose one text and prepare to read it in an inappropriate way. They should practise with a partner for a while in preparation for the guessing game.

6. Now begin the guessing game: number the groups, A, B, C, and so on. Number each member of the group, 1, 2, 3, 4. Begin with Group A, and ask them to nominate a learner from another group (e.g. C,1). Learner 1 for Group C then reads his/her extract and Group A, working together, must guess the style intended. If they guess correctly, they gain one point. If they do not, no points are awarded. The teacher adjudicates and awards a point if the speaker was unclear. The turn then passes to Group B to nominate another learner, and so on. The winner is the team with most points at the end of an allotted time or number of turns.

Sample teaching material

Fairy story

Read this as though to a small child.

Once there was a poor widow who lived in a cottage with her son Jack. One day, she said to him, 'We have no money. You must go to the market and sell the cow.' Well, on the way, Jack met a man who persuaded him to exchange the cow for some beans. Jack's mother was so angry when she heard what had happened that she threw the beans out of the window. But, what do you suppose happened? The beans grew and grew into a huge beanstalk, right up to the sky. Jack climbed up the beanstalk, and at the top there was a castle. Jack opened the door, Cre-e-e-ek! Inside there was a wicked-looking giant. Jack quickly hid in a cupboard. 'Fee-fi-fo-fum. I smell the blood of an Englishman,' said the giant. In the room there was a golden harp and a magic hen. 'Lay!' said the giant, and the hen laid an egg of gold. 'Sing!' said the giant, and the harp sang so sweetly that the giant was soon fast asleep. Then, Jack crept out of the cupboard, snatched up the harp and the hen, and ran home as fast as his legs would carry him . . .

Extract from a play

Mark Antony's speech from 'Julius Caesar' by William Shakespeare –
Read this as though you are on a large stage, playing to a large
audience.

Friends, Romans, countrymen, lend me your ears;
I come to bury Caesar, not to praise him.
The evil that men do lives after them;
The good is oft interrèd with their bones;
So let it be with Caesar. The noble Brutus
Hath told you Caesar was ambitious.
If it were so, it was a grievous fault;
And grievously hath Caesar answer'd it.
Here, under leave of Brutus and the rest –
For Brutus is an honourable man;
So are they all, all honourable men –
Come I to speak in Caesar's funeral.
He was my friend, faithful and just to me;
But Brutus says he was ambitious,
And Brutus is an honourable man . . .

News report[1]

Read this as
though you are
a newsreader
on television.

Did you see UFOs?

WITNESSES are being urged to come forward after
unidentified flying objects were spotted in the sky
over Hemlock Stone, near Stapleford.
  Mr Anthony James, organiser of East Midlands
UFO Research Association, said he received three
sightings of strange objects between 7.30pm and 7am
during March 28 to 29.
  The sitings were from two independent witnesses
living within half a mile of each other.
  Mr James said: "The objects displayed manoeuvres
not characteristic of normal aircraft."
  Anyone with more information should contact the
association on Nottingham 275623

Teacher's diary

How successful were the learners at switching intonation style? Was it
easier for them to hear this than to produce it?

Note
1. From *Nottingham Weekly Recorder and Post*, Issue 537, 16 April 1992.

52 Improving the flow

Level   Intermediate to advanced

Students   Teenage to adult

Groups   Individuals or pairs

Purpose   To improve learners' fluency, stress placement, intonation and use of weak forms

Text type   Teacher's newspaper report

In this activity

Students mark texts for pronunciation features in order to increase oral fluency.

Preparation

Choose a text of a suitable level for your learners or use the Sample teaching material.

Procedure

1. Ask your learners to read the text to themselves once or twice. Then ask them to underline the words which would be stressed – these are the ones which are essential for meaning. When listed one after the other, these important words will sound like a telegram which summarises the text. As a general rule, learners should be encouraged to mark no more than one third of all the words in the text, otherwise it will sound too heavily stressed. For the Sample teaching material text, the 'telegram' words might be:

> WITNESSES – UNIDENTIFIED FLYING OBJECTS – HEMLOCK STONE – STAPLEFORD – ANTHONY JAMES – ORGANISER UFO RESEARCH – THREE SIGHTINGS – 7.30PM 7AM – MARCH 28TH 29TH – TWO INDEPENDENT – HALF A MILE – NOT NORMAL – INFORMATION – CONTACT NOTTINGHAM 275623

2. Now ask your learners to read their 'telegram' words aloud. Check pronunciation.

3. Working in pairs, learners now read the complete text to each other. They should stress *only* the words they have underlined and they should not pause for breath except at commas and full stops. Monitor the pairs as they work.

Follow-up activities

1. Consider with your learners the relationship of new information (stressed, falling tone) to information which is old or assumed known (less stress, rising tone). In the Sample teaching material, examples of stresses on new and old information are:

Paragraph one: unidentified flying objects (new) were spotted in the sky (old – of course they were in the sky if flying).

Paragraph two: Mr. Anthony James (new), organiser of East Midlands UFO Research Association (in parenthesis so incidental information), said he received three (new – we didn't know the number before) sightings of strange objects (old – already mentioned) between 7.30pm and 7am during March 28 to 29 (new). The sightings were from two independent (new) witnesses (old – mentioned before) living within half a mile of each other (new information).

2. Consider with your learners the relationship of weak vowels to unstressed syllables. Invite them to look at the words that they have *not* chosen as 'important' in the main activity. How many of these can have weak vowels? Learners can underline or circle them in the text, then practise reading the text again. The following text shows the Sample teaching material, marked for weak /ə/ vowels.

Witnesses ə being urged tə come forwəd aftər unidentified flying objects wə spotted in thə sky ovə Hemlock Stone near Staplefəd.

Mistər Anthəny James, orgənisər əf East Midlənds UFO Research əssociatən said he received three sightings əf strange objects between 7.30pm ənd 7am during March 28 tə 29.

Thə sightings wə frəm two independənt witnesses living within half ə mile əf each othə.

Mistə James said, The objects displayed mənoeuvəs not charəctəristic əf norməl aircraft.

Anyone with more infəmatən shəd contact the əssociatən on Nottinghəm 275623.

Sample teaching material

Use the news report from Activity 51, 'Monologue restyle'.

Teacher's diary

Did this activity help the students improve their fluency in reading? Did you try either of the follow-up activities? Which were the main problems encountered by your students?

53 Intonation bodyline

Level	Elementary
Students	Young learners
Groups	Whole class
Purpose	To help learners to communicate through intonation alone, represented here by body movements
Text type	Teacher's chosen dialogue from the learners' own course book

In this activity

Learners play a guessing game based on 'walking' a dialogue.

Preparation

Choose a short dialogue which you are currently working on with your class. A taped dialogue is best because it can be played and replayed without variation, and this facilitates the imitation phase of this activity. A sample dialogue is given as teaching material.

Procedure

1. Play the tape of your chosen dialogue, or read it. Check that students have understood its meaning. Divide the class into two halves, one half taking Role A and the other Role B. Play or read the dialogue again, asking your learners to repeat their part after your model of it, miming the intonation in this way: both arms together stretching above heads and down towards the ground for falling intonation, and both arms together raised slowly upwards for rising intonation; for example:

I'd like a sweater, please.

Then ask your learners to keep the same parts and perform the dialogue themselves, in chorus. Conduct this, and convey appropriate intonation with hand gestures.

2. Now explain to the class that they are going to 'walk' their parts. Demonstrate the first few lines yourself: take a stride for each syllable – a heavy stride for the main stress and lighter ones for all the rest. Keep the hand gestures for intonation as before.

3. Play the tape again and walk it through with the class. If there is not enough space for you all to perform the walking mime at once, have single learners perform a line each with you; for example:

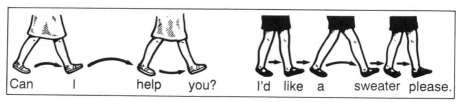

4. When the class is used to walking the lines, begin the guessing game. Invite one of the Role A students to choose any one line from their part and demonstrate it for the Role B learners to guess. The turn then passes to the B learner who guessed correctly and he/she performs one of her/his lines by 'walking' it for the A learners to guess, and so on.

Sample teaching material

A: Can I help you?

B: I'd like a sweater, please.

A: Which size would you like? Small, medium or large?

B: Medium please.

A: How about this one Sir?

B: That's perfect. Thank you.

Teacher's diary

How far were the learners able to 'keep in step' with the dialogue?
Were they able to synchronise hand gestures with intonation patterns?
Was the guessing game successful? Would you change anything in the
procedures for next time?

54 I know what you said, but what did you mean?

Level	Advanced
Students	Adults
Groups	Individual, pairs, groups or whole class
Purpose	To show learners how intonation alters meaning
Text type	Set of sentences marked for intonation

In this activity

Students choose, from two alternatives, the correct meaning of sentences.

Preparation

Use the Sample teaching material or devise your own.[1] You will need a copy for each learner, or one copy between two if learners are to work in pairs. Record the material on tape.

Procedure

1. Tell your learners that you are going to play a tape of/read out a set of sentences. They should choose which meaning, a) or b), they think is most likely.

2. Give out the worksheet for the learners to mark.

3. At the end of the reading/tape recording, before giving the correct answers, invite learners to check with each other what they have marked.

4. Now ask pairs of learners to read the sentences to each other in two ways, first with meaning a) and then with meaning b).

5. With the whole class, discuss how the sentences can be said and what they can mean.

Sample teaching material

Students' worksheet

1. a) The speaker is stating that this is the end.
   b) The speaker is asking whether this is the end.

2. a) She isn't dating anyone.
   b) She's choosy about who she dates.

3. a) I don't give the orders, I just do what I'm told.
   b) I don't work anywhere else.

4. a) The speaker is asking you to leave Henry alone.
   b) The speaker is asking Henry not to stop.

5. a) Not the other one.
   b) She has sold one of them.

6. a) If you offered him money he wouldn't do the job.
   b) Even if you offered him money he still wouldn't do the job.

7. a) I haven't been outside the house today, all because of you.
   b) You're asking why I didn't go out? Well, it's because I was expecting you to come to the house.

8. a) The speaker is offering biscuits or cake.
   b) The speaker is offering biscuits or cake or something else.

9. a) She fed the fish on cake.
   b) She took some food which was a type of cake made of fish.

10. a) The speaker is sure my name is John.
    b) The speaker isn't quite sure of my name.

Sentences with key

1. This is the end of the book.

2. She doesn't go out with any boy.

3. I only work here.

4. Don't stop Henry.

5. She says that one's sold.

6. He wouldn't do it if you paid him.

7. I didn't go out because I thought you'd come round.

8. Would you like biscuits or cake?

9. She took the fish cake.

10. Your name's John, isn't it?

Key

1. b)   2. b)   3. b)   4. b)   5. a)   6. a)   7. b)   8. b)   9. a)
10. a)

Teacher's diary

How accurate were the students in picking out the correct meanings?
Were they able to produce the appropriate intonation themselves?

Note

1.   See Madalena Cruz Ferreira, 'Testing Non-Native Intonation' in IRAL, Vol. XXVII/I
     (February 1989), pp. 35–39.

APPENDICES

Appendix 1: Diagnosis of student errors

Initial diagnosis

Both Swan and Smith, and Ann Baker (see Further reading in the Introduction to this book) give a diagnostic 'shopping list' to be read aloud by students. These lists contain all the phonemes of English and, as the student reads from his/her copy, you underline the sounds he/she mispronounces. You thus have a list of sounds to work on with the student. Alternatively, you can devise your own quick 'shopping list' from the list of words given below under More detailed diagnosis. It is also a good idea to ask the student for some unstructured and unprepared speaking, such as telling a story based on picture prompts, or general conversation with you about home and family. This unprepared speech will tell you whether the student is mispronouncing sounds which he/she *can* pronounce correctly when concentrating on reading aloud. If you record the student performing both kinds of task you will be able to analyse the errors at your leisure.

More detailed diagnosis

Having noted the sounds which cause most problems, you might want to find out whether the student can *hear* the problem sound, or whether the problem is merely one of *production*. To test this, you could read pairs of words ('minimal pairs', i.e. words which differ in one phoneme only, are to be found in plenty in Ann Baker and in O'Connor and Fletcher, see Further reading). Ask the student to mark whether each word in the pair contains the *same* sound or a *different* sound. Below is an example of a discrimination exercise for /s/ and /z/; /i/ and /ɪ/; and /əʊ/ and /ɒ/ or /ɔɪ/.

Transcript		*Answers*	
1. said / said	6. sit / seat	1. same	6. different
2. sip / zip	7. cheek / chick	2. different	7. different
3. buzz / buzz	8. ship / ship	3. same	8. same
4. peas / peace	9. cot / coat	4. different	9. different
5. bean / bean	10. soil / sole	5. same	10. different

Part of a more detailed analysis might concentrate on finding out whether the sound causes equal difficulty in all positions. Below is a list of sample words for each possible position of the phonemes of English. Learners can be asked to read or repeat them, alone or in sentences.

Consonants

Voiceless

/p/	pie, apple, cup
/t/	top, potato, cat
/f/	fir, telephone, wife
/k/	cup, biscuit, lock
/s/	sun, bicycle, glass
/ʃ/	shoe, wishing, fish
/θ/	thumb, bathroom, path
/h/	hat, ahead
/tʃ/	chicken, picture, peach

Voiced

/b/	boy, rabbit, rib
/d/	dog, idea, bud
/v/	veil, river, leave
/g/	go, digger, bag
/z/	zebra, scissors
/ʒ/	gigolo, pleasure, rouge
/ð/	the, leather, smooth
/j/	yellow, onion
/l/	lip, yellow, call
/m/	man, woman, come
/n/	now, winner, can
/r/	run, barrow
/w/	win, sandwich
/ŋ/	sing, singer
/dʒ/	jelly, soldier, bridge

Vowels

Pure vowels

/ɑ/	arm, star
/æ/	at, cat
/ɛ/	egg, bread
/ɪ/	it, pig, pretty
/i/	eat, feed, free
/ɒ/	otter, hot
/ɔ/	organ, moored, four
/ʊ/	put
/u/	moon, zoo

Diphthongs/triphthonge

/aɪ/	ice, kite
/aʊ/	owl, house
/ɛɪ/	age, cake, away
/ɛə/	air, bear, bearing
/ɪə/	earring, beard, clear
/əʊ/	owing, nowhere, pillow
/ɔɪ/	oil, noisy, boy
/ʊə/	tourist, sure
/ɜ/	early, turkey, her
/ʌ/	up, cup
/ə/	among, counsellor, father

Priorities for improving pronunciation

Frequency of phonemes is an important factor in deciding what aspects of pronunciation to concentrate on. If you look at the chart of frequencies of phonemes in Activity 22, you will see that certain phonemes of English occur up to ten times more frequently than others. We have also said, in the Introduction to Section II, that more variation is tolerated in vowels than in consonants. If a learner is unfortunate enough to mispronounce a consonant of high frequency, he/she stands more chance of being misunderstood than someone who mispronounces a vowel of low frequency. Your first priority should be, therefore, to try to correct mispronunciations of frequent sounds. However, it will be very discouraging for learners to work exclusively on sounds they find most difficult, such as a distinction which does not exist in their mother tongue (e.g. /p/ and /b/ in Arabic or /p/ and /f/ in Indonesian). From the point of view of your own and of your students' morale, you should also work on sounds which can be improved more quickly (e.g. those which your diagnosis reveals to be produced correctly *some* of the time at least).

The information in this Appendix should help you choose the sounds you will use as a basis for the work in Section II of this book. For problems with stress and intonation, the activities in Section III and IV of this book, together with Appendices 6 and 7, should provide some solutions.

Appendix 2: List of phonemic symbols[1]

Consonants

Voiceless

/p/	as in **pay**	/θ/	as in **thin**
/t/	as in **talk**	/h/	as in **hat**
/f/	as in **fit**		
/k/	as in **king**		
/s/	as in **soon**		
/ʃ/	as in **ship**		

Voiced

/b/	as in **bay**	/j/	as in **yellow**
/d/	as in **done**	/l/	as in **lip**
/v/	as in **van**	/m/	as in **mat**
/g/	as in **good**	/n/	as in **nine**
/z/	as in **zone**	/r/	as in **run**
/ʒ/	as in **gigolo**	/w/	as in **win**
/ð/	as in **this**	/ŋ/	as in **sing**

The two voiceless consonants /t/ and /ʃ/ can be made so close together that they seem to be one sound, /tʃ/, as in **cheap**. Similarly the two voiced sounds /d/ and /ʒ/ can be made so close together that they seem to be a single sound, /dʒ/, as in **judge**. Therefore, they are often classified as separate phonemes, /tʃ/ and /dʒ/.

Vowels of British English

Pure vowels

/ɑ/	as in **heart**	/ɔ/	as in **more**
/æ/	as in **hat**	/ʊ/	as in **could**
/ɛ/	as in **met**	/u/	as in **choose**
/ɪ/	as in **fit**	/ɜ/	as in **word**
/i/	as in **feed**	/ʌ/	as in **fund**
/ɒ/	as in **lost**	/ə/	as in **mother**

Diphthongs

/aɪ/	as in **cry**	/ɪə/	as in **hear**
/aʊ/	as in **out**	/əʊ/	as in **no**
/ɛɪ/	as in **say**	/ɔɪ/	as in **boy**
/ɛə/	as in **there**	/ʊə/	as in **sure**

Triphthongs

Two vowel sounds, /aɪə/ and /aʊə/, are made up of three sounds blended into one. They are therefore called 'triphthongs'.

Note
1. These are the symbols of the International Phonetic Alphabet used to represent Received Pronunciation (the standard British pronunciation) as taught by the British Council, and used in the *Collins Cobuild Dictionary*.

Appendix 3: List of words having consonant clusters

Initial clusters of two consonants

/pl/ as in **pl**ease	/gl/ as in **gl**oves	/st/ as in **st**ay
/bl/ as in **bl**ue	/kr/ as in **cr**eam	/sk/ as in **sk**y
/pr/ as in **pr**esent	/gr/ as in **gr**ey	/sm/ as in **sm**all
/br/ as in **br**other	/kw/ as in **qu**een	/sn/ as in **sn**ake
/tr/ as in **tr**avel	/fl/ as in **fl**at	/sl/ as in **sl**ow
/dr/ as in **dr**ive	/fr/ as in **fr**y	/sw/ as in **sw**eet
/tw/ as in **tw**elve	/θr/ as in **thr**ead	/ʃr/ as in **shr**ed
/kl/ as in **cl**ever	/sp/ as in **sp**eed	

Final clusters of two consonants

/pt/ as in stri**pped**	/dʒd/ as in dre**dged**	/sp/ as in wa**sp**
/ps/ as in sto**ps**	/md/ as in da**mned**	/sk/ as in whi**sk**
/ts/ as in wai**ts**	/nt/ as in wo**n't**	/ʃt/ as in wi**shed**
/kt/ as in fa**ked**	/nθ/ as in mo**nth**	/lp/ as in he**lp**
/ks/ as in so**cks**	/nz/ as in rai**ns**	/ld/ as in fi**lled**
/tʃt/ as in i**tched**	/ndʒ/ as in si**nge**	/lk/ as in si**lk**
/mp/ as in da**mp**	/ŋk/ as in ri**nk**	/lf/ as in e**lf**
/mz/ as in thu**mbs**	/ŋz/ as in thi**ngs**	/lθ/ as in stea**lth**
/nd/ as in e**nd**	/lt/ as in wi**lt**	/ft/ as in ra**ft**
/ns/ as in o**nce**	/ldʒ/ as in bu**lge**	/fθ/ as in fi**fth**
/ntʃ/ as in i**nch**	/lm/ as in fi**lm**	/vz/ as in li**ves**
/ŋd/ as in ri**nged**	/lv/ as in de**lve**	/ðd/ as in loa**thed**
/bd/ as in ro**bbed**	/lz/ as in nai**ls**	/ðz/ as in tee**thes**
/bz/ as in ro**bs**	/vd/ as in li**ved**	/st/ as in wai**st**
/dz/ as in ri**des**	/fs/ as in lau**ghs**	/zd/ as in suppo**sed**
/gd/ as in wa**gged**	/θt/ as in ba**thed**	/ʒd/ as in gara**ged**
/gz/ as in fi**gs**	/θs/ as in my**ths**	

Initial clusters of three consonants

/spl/   as in **splendid**   /skr/   as in **scream**
/spr/   as in **sprain**   /skw/   as in **squirm**
/str/   as in **strain**

Final clusters of three consonants

/pts/   as in **transcripts**   /pst/   as in **lapsed**
/pθs/   as in **depths**   /tθs/   as in **widths**
/tst/   as in **midst**   /kts/   as in **pacts**
/ksθ/   as in **sixth**   /kst/   as in **next**
/mpt/   as in **prompt**   /mps/   as in **mumps**
/mft/   as in **triumphed**   /mfs/   as in **triumphs**
/nts/   as in **ants**   /ndz/   as in **ends**
/nθs/   as in **months**   /nst/   as in **sensed**
/ntʃt/   as in **lunched**   /ndʒd/ as in **changed**
/ŋkt/   as in **thanked**   /ŋks/   as in **thinks**
/lpt/   as in **helped**   /lkt/   as in **balked**
/lps/   as in **helps**   /lts/   as in **wilts**
/lks/   as in **silks**   /lbz/   as in **bulbs**
/ldz/   as in **worlds**   /ltʃt/   as in **filched**
/ldʒd/ as in **divulged**   /lmd/   as in **filmed**
/lmz/   as in **films**   /lfs/   as in **sylphs**
/lfθ/   as in **twelfth**   /lvd/   as in **delved**
/lvz/   as in **elves**   /lθs/   as in **wealths**
/lst/   as in **whilst**   /fts/   as in **lifts**
/fθs/   as in **fifths**   /sps/   as in **wasps**
/sts/   as in **waists**   /spt/   as in **rasped**
/skt/   as in **whisked**   /sks/   as in **whisks**

Appendix 4: The phonemes of English and how they are spelt

Voiceless consonants		Voiced consonants	
Sound	*Spelling*	*Sound*	*Spelling*
/p/	p as in **drop** pp as in **dropped**	/b/	b as in **rob** bb as in **robbed**
/t/	t as in **table** tt as in **fitter** th as in **Thomas**	/d/	d as in **dove** dd as in **add**
/f/	f as in **fish** ff as in **puff** ph as in **photo** gh as in **rough**	/v/	v as in **love** f as in **of**
/k/	k as in **king** c as in **come** cc as in **accurate** ch as in **stomach** q as in **conquer**	/g/	g as in **go** gg as in **bigger** gh as in **ghost** gu as in **guess**
/s/	s as in **spell** ss as in **hiss** c as in **ceiling** sc as in **science**	/z/	z as in **zoo** zz as in **fizzy** s as in **rose**
/ʃ/	sh as in **should** ch as in **machine** s as in **sugar** ss as in **assure** ti as in **station** sci as in **conscious**	/ʒ/	si as in **vision** s as in **pleasure** z as in **azure** g as in **garage**

	ci as in spe**ci**al ce as in o**ce**an		
/θ/	th as in **th**in	/ð/	th as in **th**is
/h/	h as in **h**at wh as in **wh**o	/j/	y as in **y**es i as in on**i**on
/tʃ/	ch as in **ch**in tch as in wa**tch** t as in na**t**ure	/l/	l as in **l**ight ll as in fi**ll**
		/m/	m as in **m**oon mm as in sli**mm**ing mb as in thu**mb** mn as in da**mn**
		/n/	n as in **n**o nn as in wi**nn**er gn as in **gn**ome kn as in **kn**ee pn as in **pn**eumatic
		/r/	r as in **r**ain rr as in te**rr**ible wr as in **wr**ite rh as in **rh**yme
		/w/	w as in **w**et wh as in **wh**ich o as in **o**ne u as in s**u**ite
		/ŋ/	ng as in si**ng** n as in tha**n**k
		/dʒ/	g as in **g**em j and dg as in **j**u**dg**e dj as in a**dj**acent gg as in su**gg**est di as in sol**di**er

Pure Vowels		Diphthongs	
Sound	*Spelling*	*Sound*	*Spelling*
/ɑ/	a as in **father** ar as in **car** al as in **calm** ear as in **heart** au as in **laugh** er as in **clerk**	/aɪ/	i as in **time** igh as in **high** ie as in **lie** y as in **cry**
/æ/	a as in **hat**	/aʊ/	ou as in **house** ow as in **now**
/ɛ/	e as in **bed** ea as in **breath** a as in **many**	/ɛɪ/	a as in **hate** ei as in **eight** ey as in **prey** ai as in **rain** ay as in **ray**
/ɪ/	i as in **sit** e and y as in **pretty** ie as in **sieve** u as in **busy** o as in **women** a as in **village**	/ɛə/	air as in **chair** are as in **pare** ear as in **wear**
/i/	ee as in **cheese** ea as in **pea** e as in **be** ie as in **piece** ei as in **receive** ey as in **key** i as in **machine**	/ɪə/	eer as in **deer** ear as in **fear** ere as in **here** ea as in **idea** ier as in **pier**
/ɒ/	o as in **dog** a as in **swan** au as in **because**	/əʊ/	o as in **so** oa as in **road** oe as in **toe**

	ou as in **c<u>ou</u>gh** ow as in **kn<u>ow</u>ledge**		ou as in **alth<u>ou</u>gh** ow as in **l<u>ow</u>** ew as in **s<u>ew</u>**
/ɔ/	or as in **f<u>or</u>d** a as in **f<u>a</u>ll** aw as in **<u>aw</u>ful** au as in **d<u>au</u>ghter** ou as in **<u>ou</u>ght** oar as in **h<u>oar</u>d** oor as in **fl<u>oor</u>**	/ɔɪ/	oi as in **n<u>oi</u>se** oy as in **b<u>oy</u>**
/ʊ/	u as in **f<u>u</u>ll** ou as in **c<u>ou</u>ld** oo as in **f<u>oo</u>t** o as in **w<u>o</u>man**	/ʊə/	oor as in **p<u>oor</u>** our as in **t<u>our</u>** ure as in **s<u>ure</u>**
/u/	oo as in **t<u>oo</u>** ou as in **y<u>ou</u>** o as in **t<u>o</u>**		
/ɜ/	ur as in **ch<u>ur</u>ch** ir as in **g<u>ir</u>l** er as in **h<u>er</u>s** ear as in **h<u>ear</u>d** or as in **w<u>or</u>ld** our as in **j<u>our</u>ney**		
/ʌ/	u as in **s<u>u</u>n** o as in **s<u>o</u>n** ou as in **c<u>ou</u>sin** oo as in **bl<u>oo</u>d** oe as in **d<u>oe</u>s**		
/ə/	too numerous to mention – see Appendix 5: Weak forms		

Appendix 5: Weak forms

a	Give me <u>a</u> kiss.
an	Eat <u>an</u> apple.
and	Fish <u>and</u> chips.
are	What <u>are</u> we doing tomorrow?*
at	I'll see you <u>at</u> nine.
but	I would if I could <u>but</u> I can't.
can	I <u>can</u> do anything better than you.*
could	The doctor <u>could</u> see you tomorrow.*
do	What <u>do</u> you want?*
does	What <u>does</u> she want?*
for	Come over <u>for</u> tea.
from	It's a letter <u>from</u> Tim.
her	I haven't seen <u>her</u> since Monday.*
had	If only Max <u>had</u> seen her, . . .*
has	What <u>has</u> happened?*
have	What <u>have</u> you done?*
just	I've <u>just</u> done it.
of	He's one <u>of</u> us.
shall	What <u>shall</u> I do with it?*
should	What <u>should</u> I do with it?*
some	Would you like <u>some</u> coffee?
such	I've never heard <u>such</u> a thing.
than	He's looking better <u>than</u> ever.
that	I had no idea <u>that</u> you were coming.
the	Pass <u>the</u> salt please.
them	I told <u>them</u> not to do it.*
to	We went <u>to</u> York on the train.
was	What <u>was</u> the party like?*
were	They <u>were</u> watching us.*

Note

*   It is also possible to give these forms their full vowel length if the words are being stressed for emphasis. (See the reference to 'contrastive stress' in Activity 43.)

Appendix 6: Stress rules

Below are the rules used for Activities in Section III. In general:

a) Nouns and verbs of more than two syllables ending in -vowel consonant or -vowel consonant silent 'e' have their stress on the antepenultimate syllable, e.g.

<u>fo</u>rtitude <u>de</u>tonate <u>gra</u>duate

b) Words ending in -ee, -eer, -ese, -oo, -ette, -oon have their stress on the final syllable, e.g.

refu<u>gee</u> Japa<u>nese</u> mountain<u>eer</u>

c) Words ending in -ery, -ate, -orous, -mentary, -eous have their stress on the antepenultimate syllable, e.g.

<u>for</u>tunate <u>son</u>orous compli<u>men</u>tary

d) Words ending in -ic, -ish, -ive, -ure, -ation, -mental have their stress on the penultimate syllable, e.g.

ter<u>rif</u>ic ad<u>mon</u>ish reve<u>la</u>tion

e) Weak suffixes -ly, -er (except after Greek elements), -ness, -ful, -less, -able, -ment do *not* affect stress: when a prefix or suffix of Old English origin is added to a word, it generally has no effect on stress position, e.g.

<u>ha</u>ppy, <u>ha</u>ppiness <u>co</u>lour, <u>co</u>lourless <u>nor</u>thern, <u>nor</u>therner

f) Words of Greek, Latin or Romance origin often show a *shift* of stress when a prefix or suffix is added or changed. For example, words beginning with seismo-, micro- or hexa- and continuing with -graph, -phone, -gon, -scope and so on are stressed on the first syllable, e.g.

<u>seis</u>mograph <u>micro</u>scope <u>hexa</u>gon

If then a bound ending such as -y, -er, -al, -our is also added, then the stress shifts to the second syllable, e.g.

seis<u>mo</u>grapher mi<u>cro</u>scopy hex<u>ag</u>onal

The reader is referred to Kreidler, p. 87 and pp. 199–218 for a full explanation of stress rules and its relationship to syntax, morphology and phonology.

Appendix 7: Intonation rules of thumb

Learners of English often complain that they find it difficult to converse with native speakers of English. Part of the problem might be that they are focussing too much on *conversing* (i.e. talking). By paying more attention to *responding* (i.e. listening and sounding interested), they would make life much easier for themselves. The native speaker would be encouraged to say more, and the learner would therefore need to say less. Here are a few simple rules and procedures to help learners keep a conversation going.

1. Vocal range

To sound enthusiastic or interested, learners need to use a very wide vocal range. Compare Version 1 with the same conversation in Version 2.

Version 1

A: I went to the sales in town yesterday.

B: Really?
A: Yes and I got some great bargains.

B: Oh, that's wonderful.
A: (Silence. Native speaker thinks learner is bored and stops talking.)

Version 2

A: I went to the sales in town yesterday.

B: Really?
A: Yes and I got some great bargains.

B: Oh, that's wonderful.
A: It is, isn't it? I'm really thrilled.
   (Native speaker thinks learner is sympathetic and carries on.)

2. English tones

The two main tones are falling (↘) and rising (↗). Within the falling category there is a second tone, the rise-fall (↗↘) and within the rising category there is also a second tone, the fall-rise (↘↗). I would advise foreign learners of English to avoid the rise-fall altogether because it can easily sound sarcastic, and it is rare in any case. I would also advise them to be sparing in their use of the simple rising tone, which can sound arrogant, and, instead, to cultivate the fall-rise. I cannot stress enough the positive effect of the fall-rise tone – 'the friendly tone'. It means, 'We both know about this, so we understand each other' or 'I would really value your opinion about this' or 'Please say more'. A speaker who uses too many straight falling tones can sound abrupt and aggressive, so I would advise adding an extra word or two just to turn the simple fall into a fall-rise; for example:

A: Where are you from?

B: Canada. ↘
A: Really? Which part exactly?

B: Winnipeg. ↘

A: Where are you from?

B: Canada, ↘ actually. ↗
A: Really? Which part exactly?

B: Winnipeg, ↘ as a matter of fact. ↗

General rules or 'tendencies'

A falling tone is used:
- When the speaker is sure of his/her information

  e.g. You're from Canada, ↘ aren't you? ↘
- When the speaker is asking a 'question word' question, for the first time

  e.g. Where are you from? ↘

  Who did you see? ↘

  How much did you pay? ↘

A rising tone is used:

- When the speaker is unsure of him/herself

  e.g. She's from Canada, I think.
- When the speaker needs an answer from his/her hearer

  e.g. You're from Canada, aren't you?
- When the speaker is asking a 'yes/no' question

  e.g. Are you from Canada?

  Did you see her?
- When the speaker is checking information (e.g. asking a 'question word' question for the second time)

  e.g. Where did you say you were from?

Appendix 8: Expected pronunciation difficulties according to language background

1. African languages

Vowels

Confusion of /i/ and /ɪ/; /e/ and /ɜ/; /æ/, /ɑ/ and /ʌ/; /ʊ/ and /u/; /ɒ/, /ɔ/ and /əʊ/; weak vowels.

Consonants

Confusion of /l/ and /r/;
/ð/, /θ/, /ŋ/, final voiced consonants, final consonant clusters.

Stress

African speakers tend to stress the antepenultimate syllable in a word. They should be shown that stress can vary.

Intonation

These speakers tend to use a low fall rather too much. They should be shown how to use a high fall and a fall-rise.

2. Arabic

Vowels

All short vowels.

Consonants

Confusion of /g/, /dʒ/ and /k/; /p/ and /b/; /v/ and /f/;
/h/, /r/, /ð/, /θ/, /g/, overuse of glottal stop.

Stress

Arabic speakers are unfamiliar with grammatical stress. They should be shown that the same word may have first *or* second syllable stressed (e.g. 'permit', 'permit').

Intonation

As for African languages.

3. Chinese

Vowels

Confusion of /i/ and /ɪ/; /u/ and /ʊ/;
/æ/, /ɒ/, /ʌ/, diphthongs too short, weak forms.

Consonants

Confusion of /n/ and /l/; /l/ and /r/;
/b/, /d/, /g/, /v/, /θ/, /ð/, /h/, /z/, /dʒ/, /tʃ/, /ʃ/, consonant clusters.

Intonation

Chinese speakers tend to have a fixed intonation pattern, and need to be shown how stress can vary to alter meaning.

4. French

Vowels

Confusion of /i/ and /ɪ/; /ʊ/ and /u/; /ɔ/ and /əʊ/;
/ʌ/, /æ/, /ei/, weak forms.

Consonants

/θ/, /ð/, /tʃ/, /h/, /r/, /z/.

Stress

French speakers are unfamiliar with contrastive stress, and need to be shown how emphasis can be shown by stress alone, not by a change in word order.

Intonation

These speakers need to be shown how to make a glide from high to low pitch, or from low to high pitch, over a single syllable.

5. German

Vowels

Confusion of /e/ and /æ/; /ɔ/ and /əʊ/;
/ei/, weak forms.

Consonants

Confusion of /v/ and /w/;
/ʒ/, /dʒ/, /ʃ/, /tʃ/, /θ/, /ð/, /r/.

Intonation

German speakers tend to use too many simple rising tones, which make them sound arrogant. They need to cultivate a fall-rise.

6. Greek

Vowels

Confusion of /i/ and /ɪ/; /æ/ and /e/; /ɜ/, /ə/ and /e/; /ɒ/, /əʊ/ and /ɔ/;
/ʌ/, weak forms.

Consonants

Confusion of /ʃ/ and /s/; /ʒ/ and /z/; /ŋ/ and /ŋg/; /tʃ/ and /ʃ/; /dʒ/ and /ʒ/.

Stress

Greek speakers need to be shown that a single word may have more than one stressed syllable.

Intonation

These speakers use the high fall too often and need to be shown the low fall and fall-rise.

7. Indian languages

Vowels

Confusion of /e/ and /æ/; /ɒ/, /ɔ/ and /ɑ/; /eɪ/ and /e/; /aɪ/ and /ɔɪ/; /əʊ/, weak forms.

Consonants

Confusion of /θ/ and /t/; /ð/ and /d/; /s/ and /ʃ/; /p/, /t/, /k/, /d/, /ʒ/ clusters.

Stress

Speakers of Indian languages need to be shown that stress can shift, both within a single word, and within a phrase.

Intonation

These speakers can vary pitch, but need to be shown that loudness and length should also be used to vary stress.

8. Italian

Vowels

Confusion of /i/ and /ɪ/; /æ/ and /e/; /əʊ/, weak vowels.

Consonants

/θ/, /ð/, /ʒ/, /ŋ/, /h/, confusion of /s/ and /z/, final consonants given a schwa, clusters.

Stress

Italian speakers need to be shown that stress shift can alter meaning.

Intonation

These speakers need to be shown how attitude can be conveyed through intonation.

9. Japanese

Vowels

Confusion of /ɔ/, /əʊ/ and /ɒ/; /æ/, /ʌ/ and /ɑ/; /ɜ/ and /ɑ/;
/ɪ/, /ʊ/, /u/.

Consonants

Confusion of /l/ and /r/; /h/ and /f/; /v/ and /b/; /g/ and /ŋ/; /t/ and /tʃ/; /d/ and /dʒ/;
/s/ and /z/; /t/ and /ts/, /θ/, /ð/.

Intonation

Japanese speakers need to be shown how intonation is used to highlight the difference between what is given and what is new.

10. Portuguese

Vowels

Confusion of /i/ and /ɪ/; /e/ and /æ/; /ɒ/ and /ɔ/; /ʊ/ and /u/; /ʌ/ and /æ/; weak vowels.

Consonants

Aspiration, confusion of /tʃ/ and /ʃ/; /dʒ/ and /ʒ/;
/h/, /θ/, /ð/, clusters.

Stress

Portuguese speakers need to be shown how stress shift works.

Intonation

These speakers often use too low a pitch on falling tones and they need to raise the pitch in order to sound more interested.

11. Russian

Vowels

Confusion of /a/ and /ɑ/; /æ/ and /e/;
/ɔ/, /əʊ/, /ɜ/, long vowels, /j/ inserted sometimes.

Consonants

/θ/, /ð/, /ŋ/; final /b/, /d/, /q/; confusion of /w/ and /v/, aspiration, clusters

Intonation

Russian speakers tend to overuse the falling tone for questions. They need to practise 'yes/no' questions with a rise.

12. Scandinavian languages

Vowels

Confusion of /i/ and /ɪ/; /æ/ and /e/; /ʌ/ and /ɒ/;
/ɜ/, /ʊ/, /u/, /əʊ/, weak forms.

Consonants

/θ/, /ð/, /z/, /ʒ/, /tʃ/, /dʒ/, /r/, /w/, voiced final consonants.

Stress

Speakers of Scandinavian languages tend to stress the first element in a compound. They need to be shown that the second element may sometimes carry the stress.

Intonation

Some of these speakers use too many rising tones and need to be shown how to use falls. Others have a rather narrow pitch range which needs to be widened by practising high falls and high rises.

13. Spanish

Vowels

Confusion of /i/ and /ɪ/; /æ/, /ɑ/, /ʌ/; /əʊ/, /ɔ/, /ɒ/.

Consonants

Aspiration, voiced final plosives, /t/, /k/, /p/, /z/, /r/, /h/.
Confusion of /m/ and /ŋ/; /b/ and /v/; /d/ and /ð/; /s/ and /ʃ/; /ʃ/, /tʃ/ and /dʒ/; /dʒ/ and /j/; /w/ and /gw/, clusters.

Stress

Spanish speakers have an over-even rhythm which can be monotonous. They need help with variable stress and vowel length.

Intonation

These speakers may use a pitch range which is too narrow so they need to be encouraged to use high falls and rises.

14. Turkish

Vowels

Confusion of /i/, /ɪə/ and /ɪ/; /e/ and /æ/; /ɔ/ and /əʊ/; /eə/ and /eɪ/, vowels between consonants.

Consonants

Confusion of /v/ and /w/; final /m/, /n/ and /l/; /θ/, /ð/, /r/, final /b/, /d/, /dʒ/.

Stress

Turkish speakers can be too heavy with their stress placement so they may need to be helped to tone it down.

Intonation

These speakers need to be shown how to use fall-rises.

INDEXES

Index 1: Summary of activities

Activities are listed sequentially by section

I Working with English pronunciation in context
1. *Mr Brown says, 'Yes':* Learners play a guessing game to reveal the importance of pronunciation in conveying attitude
2. *Say it with feeling:* Learners play a game involving matching voice with attitude
3. *Act English:* Learners talk about themselves in their mother tongue, using an English accent
4. *Wordless video:* Learners mime and set words to soundless video
5. *Hard sell:* Learners play the role of TV or radio advertiser
6. *Spotting contractions:* Learners listen to authentic English speech to discover where contractions occur
7. *English as she is spoke:* Learners explore elisions and assimilations, then 'find the joke' in plays-on-words
8. *Targeting:* Learners work with the teacher to monitor chosen features of their pronunciation
9. *Dialogue completion:* Learners role-play a telephone dialogue, complete a one-sided dialogue, and transcribe other learners' dialogues
10. *'Tell me' games:* Learners dictate to each other in gamelike fashion
11. *Human computer:* Learners improve pronunciation of their own perceived difficulties
12. *Read my lips:* Learners play a guessing game, matching their partner's lip shapes to words from a list

II Working with English sounds
13. *Single sound mnemonics:* Learners mime and say English sounds
14. *Describe and arrange:* Learners arrange a set of pictures according to instructions
15. *Picture–sound matching games:* Learners play card games based on matching sounds to symbols
16. *How many sounds in the picture?:* Learners find objects to illustrate a given sound
17. *Classifying sounds:* Learners place words on a grid
18. *Guess my list:* Learners play a game involving selecting items with given phonemes
19. *Phonemic script team game:* Learners play a game involving recognition of phonemic symbols
20. *Odd sound out:* Learners circle the 'odd one out' in given lists of words
21. *Sound puzzles:* Learners complete a crossword or wordsearch
22. *Phonemic scrabble:* Learners play a board game involving phonemic symbols
23. *Sound ladders:* Learners connect visuals or movements with sounds
24. *Memory game:* Learners play a memory game of increasing difficulty
25. *Sounds travel game:* Learners play a game based on a map of an English speaking country

26. *Information gap shopping list:* Learners work in pairs to ask for information, whilst practising targeted sounds
27. *Can I come to the party?:* Learners play a communication game based on tongue twisters
28. *The yes/no game:* Learners play an elimination game based on sound discrimination

III Working with English rhyme and rhythm
29. *The cat sat on the mat:* Learners volunteer rhyming words
30. *Rhyme sets/rhyme pairs:* Learners compete to find a number of rhyming objects
31. *Rhyming work cards:* Learners complete sets of rhyming words
32. *Rhyming snap:* Learners play a card game involving matching rhymes
33. *Colour rhyme bingo:* Learners play a matching game using colour
34. *Action rhymes:* Learners recite rhymes with related actions
35. *Rapping:* Learners brainstorm words with common suffixes, then sing along with a related rap
36. *The poet speaks:* Learners look for rhymes in a poem, devise other rhymes to fit, then recite together
37. *Limerick jigsaws:* Learners reconstruct and complete limericks
38. *Compound word stress:* Learners practise varying stress to alter meaning
39. *Guess the stress:* Learners engage in a communicative matching activity
40. *Stress pictures:* Learners undertake a problem-solving activity matching stress patterns to colour and shape
41. *Shifting stress dominoes:* Learners play a card game to discover stress shift rules

IV Working with English intonation
42. *I got rhythm:* Learners use dictation as a vehicle for ear training
43. *Playing with stress shift:* Learners perform a chain of responses
44. *Punctuation card game:* Learners play an elimination game to practise the relationship between intonation and punctuation
45. *Calling choices:* Learners respond to each others' questions
46. *Testing assumptions:* Learners play a question and answer game
47. *Over and over again:* Learners play a game in which they repeat information using a different form of words
48. *Highlighting picture differences:* Learners work in pairs to discover differences between two pictures
49. *Counting out an argument:* Learners act out wordless dialogues, then script them
50. *Afterthoughts:* Learners play a group question and answer game
51. *Monologue restyle:* Learners experiment with matching appropriate intonation to different genres of monologue
52. *Improving the flow:* Learners mark texts for pronunciation features in order to increase oral fluency
53. *Intonation bodyline:* Learners 'walk' a dialogue
54. *I know what you said, but what did you mean?:* Learners choose from alternatives the correct meaning of utterances

Index 2: Activities by language proficiency level

Most activities in this book can be adapted for any level. However, this index indicates activities particularly suited to a given level.

Index 3: Activities by student type

Most activities can be adapted to learners of all ages but those most suited to a particular age group are listed below.